D1106084

# OECD *Economic Surveys*
# Electronic Books

The OECD, recognising the strategic role of electronic publishing, will be issuing the OECD *Economic Surveys*, both for the Member countries and for countries of Central and Eastern Europe covered by the Organisation's Centre for Co-operation with Economies in Transition, as electronic books with effect from the 1994/1995 series -- incorporating the text, tables and figures of the printed version. The information will appear on screen in an identical format, including the use of colour in graphs.

The electronic book, which retains the quality and readability of the printed version throughout, will enable readers to take advantage of the new tools that the ACROBAT software (included on the diskette) provides by offering the following benefits:

- ❏ User-friendly and intuitive interface
- ❏ Comprehensive index for rapid text retrieval, including a table of contents, as well as a list of numbered tables and figures
- ❏ Rapid browse and search facilities
- ❏ Zoom facility for magnifying graphics or for increasing page size for easy readability
- ❏ Cut and paste capabilities
- ❏ Printing facility
- ❏ Reduced volume for easy filing/portability

*Working environment:* DOS, Windows or Macintosh.

**Subscription:**   FF 1 800   US$317   £200   DM 545

**Single issue:**   FF 130   US$24   £14   DM 40

**Complete 1994/1995 series on CD-ROM:**

FF 2 000   US$365   £220   DM 600

*Please send your order to OECD Electronic Editions or, preferably, to the Centre or bookshop with whom you placed your initial order for this Economic Survey.*

# OECD
# ECONOMIC
# SURVEYS

## 1994-1995

### FINLAND

ORGANISATION FOR ECONOMIC CO-OPERATION AND DEVELOPMENT

# ORGANISATION FOR ECONOMIC CO-OPERATION AND DEVELOPMENT

Pursuant to Article 1 of the Convention signed in Paris on 14th December 1960, and which came into force on 30th September 1961, the Organisation for Economic Co-operation and Development (OECD) shall promote policies designed:

—  to achieve the highest sustainable economic growth and employment and a rising standard of living in Member countries, while maintaining financial stability, and thus to contribute to the development of the world economy;

—  to contribute to sound economic expansion in Member as well as non-member countries in the process of economic development; and

—  to contribute to the expansion of world trade on a multilateral, non-discriminatory basis in accordance with international obligations.

The original Member countries of the OECD are Austria, Belgium, Canada, Denmark, France, Germany, Greece, Iceland, Ireland, Italy, Luxembourg, the Netherlands, Norway, Portugal, Spain, Sweden, Switzerland, Turkey, the United Kingdom and the United States. The following countries became Members subsequently through accession at the dates indicated hereafter: Japan (28th April 1964), Finland (28th January 1969), Australia (7th June 1971), New Zealand (29th May 1973) and Mexico (18th May 1994). The Commission of the European Communities takes part in the work of the OECD (Article 13 of the OECD Convention).

Publié également en français.

# Table of contents

# Boxes

# Tables

iv

*Statistical annex and structural indicators*

# Diagrams

*Text*

# BASIC STATISTICS OF FINLAND

## THE LAND

| | | | |
|---|---|---|---|
| Area (1 000 sq. km) | 338 | Population in major cities, 31.12.1991: | |
| *of which:* | | Helsinki | 497 542 |
| Cultivated land | 27 | Espoo | 175 670 |
| Forests | 187 | Tampere | 173 797 |
| Lakes | 32 | Turku | 159 403 |

## THE PEOPLE

| | | | |
|---|---|---|---|
| Total population (31.12.1993), thousands | 5 080 | Manpower by industry in 1992 (per cent of total): | |
| Per sq. km of land area | 15.0 | Agriculture and forestry | 12.5 |
| Per thousand inhabitants (1993): | | Industry and construction | 38.9 |
| Live births | 12.8 | Commerce | 21.9 |
| Deaths | 10.1 | Transport and communication | 10.4 |
| Net natural increase | 2.8 | Services | 16.3 |
| Net increase of population | 4.9 | | |

## PARLIAMENT AND GOVERNMENT

| | | | |
|---|---|---|---|
| Composition of Parliament, number of seats (1994): | | Government, number of ministers from: | |
| Center Party | 55 | Center Party | 8 |
| Social Democratic Party | 48 | National Coalition (Conservatives) | 6 |
| National Coalition (Conservatives) | 40 | Swedish People's Party | 2 |
| Left-Wing Alliance | 19 | | |
| Swedish People's Party | 12 | Total | 16 |
| Green League | 10 | | |
| Christian League | 8 | | |
| Rural Party | 7 | | |
| Liberal Party | 1 | | |
| Total | 200 | | |

## PRODUCTION

| | | | |
|---|---|---|---|
| Gross Domestic Product 1993 (Mk million) | 478 656 | Gross Domestic Product by industry in 1992 (per cent of total): | |
| GDP per head, US dollars, 1993 | 16 473 | Agriculture and forestry | 6.5 |
| Gross fixed capital formation 1993 (Mk million) | 71 272 | Industry and construction | 40.4 |
| | | Commerce | 15.6 |
| | | Transport and communication | 11.1 |
| | | Other services | 26.4 |

## PUBLIC SECTOR

| | | | |
|---|---|---|---|
| Public consumption 1993, per cent of GDP | 23.4 | General government revenue and expenditure, 1993 (Mk million) | |
| Gross fixed capital formation 1993, per cent of GDP: | | Current revenue | 257 159 |
| General government | 2.8 | Current expenditure | 284 122 |
| | | *of which:* | |
| | | Consumption | 111 955 |
| | | Transfers | 133 447 |
| | | Subsidies | 16 319 |
| | | Interest on public debt | 22 401 |

## FOREIGN TRADE

| | | | |
|---|---|---|---|
| Exports of goods and services, per cent of GDP, 1993 | 33.3 | Imports of goods and services, per cent of GDP, 1993 | 27.7 |
| Main exports in 1993 (per cent of total): | | Main imports in 1993 (per cent of total): | |
| Agricultural products | 1.3 | Raw materials | 59.2 |
| Wood products | 8.1 | Fuels and lubricants | 4.5 |
| Pulp and paper | 27.9 | Investment goods | 14.9 |
| Metal and engines | 35.9 | Consumer goods | 20.4 |
| Other goods | 26.7 | | |

## THE CURRENCY

| | | | |
|---|---|---|---|
| Monetary unit: Markka | | Currency units per US$, average of daily figures: | |
| | | Year 1993 | 5.72 |
| | | October 1993 | 4.68 |

*Note:* An international comparison of certain basic statistics is given in an annex table.

# Introduction

Finland's economy is currently rebounding from the deep slump which, from 1990 to mid-1993, saw real GDP falling by almost 15 per cent and the unemployment rate rising from 3.5 to 19 per cent. These developments originated in the conjunction of severe domestic and external shocks: the bursting of the strong credit boom of the 1980s, which provoked sharp balance-sheet adjustments in the private sector and a banking crisis; the world recession; and the collapse of trade with the former Soviet Union. As a result, both the budget and external balances deteriorated substantially and, following speculative pressure on the currency, associated with disturbances in European exchange markets, interest rates rose dramatically. After a 12 per cent devaluation in November 1991, the markka was left to float in September 1992, whereupon it depreciated by a further 20 per cent against the Ecu over the ensuing six months.

In response to these adverse shocks, the strategy followed by the Finnish authorities has been essentially to promote the emergence of a non-inflationary recovery, while restoring confidence in the currency and preserving the stability of the financial system. To this end, monetary policy has aimed at encouraging a moderate wage and price behaviour, through the announcement of a low inflation target. On the fiscal side, restrictive measures – based essentially on spending restraint – have been adopted to re-establish control over the public finance situation. At the same time, however, substantial support has been granted by the government to the banks in order to strengthen their capital and restructure their balance sheets. Finally, structural reform has been pursued with a view to both supporting economic restructuring and paving the way for Finland's participation in the European integration process.

Led by booming exports, economic activity started recovering in the second half of 1993. Current indicators signal that private consumption and investment are also picking up slightly, as households' financial position improved some-

1

what and corporate profitability in manufacturing industries increased significantly. Consequently, real GDP growth, which is estimated to have reached 3½ per cent in 1994, should accelerate during 1995-96 to around 4½ per cent on average. Reflecting this, unemployment could fall progressively, while inflation – which has hardly been affected by the substantial currency depreciation – is expected to remain subdued.

Helped by the emergence of a growing current account surplus, the markka has strengthened since early 1993, allowing the gradual easing of short-term interest rates – which began after the floating – to continue. Long-term rates also declined markedly until February 1994, when, in line with bond market developments across OECD countries, they rose significantly. Concerns about public finance developments seem to be contributing to the upward pressure on Finnish bond yields. Indeed, after a significant reduction from 7.1 per cent of GDP in 1993 to 4.7 per cent in 1994, the general government deficit is officially projected to increase to 5 per cent of GDP in 1995. As a result, the gross public debt/GDP ratio is set to continue to rise to levels above the OECD average.

Part of the pause in the fiscal consolidation process in 1995 is due to structural measures recently introduced in the field of agricultural subsidies, to prepare the ground for membership of the European Union. These measures imply a temporary increase of income support to farmers to compensate for the reduction in agricultural prices. Other major structural initiatives include the broadening and acceleration of the privatisation programme, as well as the deregulation of the telecommunication market.

Part I of the Survey reviews recent economic trends and short-term prospects. Macroeconomic and structural policies are discussed in Part II. Part III examines in some detail Finland's welfare system, with a view to identifying policy requirements in this area, designed to contain the rising cost of government welfare programmes and remove their distorting effects on the labour market. Conclusions are presented in Part V.

# I. Recent developments and short-term prospects

## An export-led recovery

Spurred by vigorous growth in exports in the wake of the fall of the markka in the early 1990s, the Finnish economy is now recovering from its longest and deepest recession in post-war history. After three years of falling output – with real GDP declining by almost 15 per cent in the period 1990-93 – overall economic growth reached $3\frac{1}{2}$ per cent in the first half of 1994 (Table 1), and the large output gap which developed in recent years has finally started to narrow (Diagram 1, Panel A). The export boom has benefited mainly manufacturing industries which, in continuation of the trend observed in 1992, saw their value added growing by $5\frac{1}{2}$ per cent in 1993 and an additional 11 per cent in the first half of 1994 (Diagram 1, Panel B). By contrast, the domestic-oriented sectors of the economy continued to weaken in 1993, with their output stabilising only in early 1994 (Diagram 1, Panel C). Most recently, though, domestic demand has shown signs of strengthening, posting positive growth rates in the first half of 1994 after bottoming at its lowest level since the early 1980s (Diagram 1, Panel E and Table 1). Indeed, while still below trend levels, both private investment and consumption appear to be reviving, as manufacturing output is approaching full capacity and consumer confidence is increasing.

With the recovery gaining momentum, seasonally-adjusted unemployment declined modestly to 18 per cent in the autumn of 1994 from its peak of 19 per cent at the beginning of the year. At the same time, wage and price inflation has remained subdued and the current account turned into surplus in early 1994. The paragraphs below review in more detail these developments before discussing the short-term outlook.

### Diagram 1.  **GDP AND ITS MAIN COMPONENTS**

Constant 1990 prices, seasonally adjusted

- - - - - - - Trends[1]

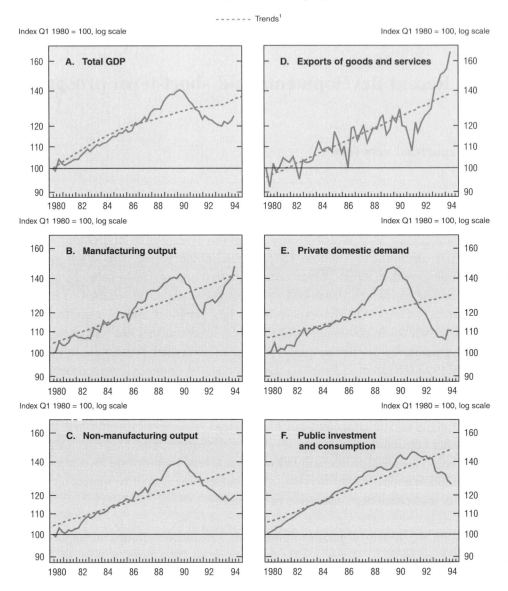

1.  For GDP the trend is derived from a production function estimated by the OECD Secretariat. For the other
variables, the trend is a linear regression line.
*Source:*  OECD, *Quarterly National Accounts.*

## Table 1. **Demand and output**

Percentage changes from previous period, seasonnally adjusted at annual rates, volume

|  | 1990 current prices Mk billion | 1991 | 1992 | 1993 | 1993: S1 | 1993: S2 | 1994: S1 |
|---|---|---|---|---|---|---|---|
| Private consumption | 269.8 | –3.6 | –4.9 | –4.0 | –5.9 | –0.7 | 3.3 |
| Government consumption | 108.5 | 2.5 | –2.2 | –5.4 | –8.5 | –2.3 | –5.5 |
| Gross fixed capital formation | 139.1 | –20.3 | –16.9 | –19.0 | –22.9 | –2.3 | 7.7 |
| *of which:* | | | | | | | |
| Public sector | 17.3 | –0.2 | –2.0 | –15.0 | –24.0 | –8.2 | –14.2 |
| Business sector | 83.5 | –24.1 | –21.0 | –22.3 | –24.5 | –15.0 | 21.6 |
| Residential | 38.4 | –20.7 | –16.1 | –14.2 | –18.5 | 5.6 | –2.0 |
| Final domestic demand | 517.4 | –6.8 | –7.1 | –6.7 | –9.8 | –2.6 | 2.0 |
| Stockbuilding [1] | 5.8 | –1.6 | 1.4 | 0.4 | 0.2 | 2.0 | –0.7 |
| Total domestic demand | 523.2 | –8.3 | –5.7 | –6.3 | –9.6 | –0.5 | 1.3 |
| Exports of goods and services | 118.8 | –6.6 | 10.0 | 16.6 | 22.5 | 11.6 | 12.3 |
| Imports of goods and services | 126.6 | –11.7 | 1.1 | 0.3 | 2.5 | 2.1 | 6.7 |
| Foreign balance [1] | – | 1.4 | 2.1 | 4.3 | 5.8 | 3.1 | 2.3 |
| GDP | 515.4 | –7.1 | –3.6 | –2.0 | –3.8 | 2.6 | 3.5 |
| *Memorandum item:* | | | | | | | |
| GDP, OECD – Europe | | 1.5 | 1.2 | –0.1 | –0.5 | 1.5 | 2.7 |

1. Contribution to GDP growth.
*Source:* OECD Secretariat.

## Strong export performance

During 1993, exports continued to increase rapidly, in spite of stagnant growth in Finland's traditional export markets in OECD-Europe. Exports of manufactured goods – which represent almost 95 per cent of Finnish sales abroad – outstripped market growth by almost 20 percentage points (Table 2). This reflects mainly the competitiveness gains associated with the depreciation of the exchange rate prior to mid-1993, and a fall in relative unit labour cost – itself resulting from rapid productivity growth and wage moderation (Diagram 2). Preliminary data suggest that export growth rates have slowed somewhat in the first half of 1994, despite a pickup in market growth. This may reflect emerging capacity constraints in the export sector. Cost-competitiveness of Finnish exports is still strong, however, even though the markka has been steadily appreciating against all major currencies since early 1993 (see Part II). This is due to the fact that, after their considerable fall in 1991/92, unit labour costs, in local currency terms, have remained largely stable.

5

## Table 2. **Export performance**

Percentage changes from previous period, seasonally adjusted at annual rates, volume

|  | 1990 Mk billion | 1991 | 1992 | 1993 | 1993: S1 | 1993: S2 | 1994: S1 |
|---|---|---|---|---|---|---|---|
| Manufacturing products | 88.3 | | | | | | |
| Export growth | | −12.1 | 9.8 | 18.9 | 24.6 | 20.4 | 8.2 |
| Market growth | | 1.1 | 2.8 | 0.3 | −3.8 | 8.1 | 11.0 |
| Export performance[1] | | −13.1 | 6.9 | 18.6 | 29.5 | 11.4 | −2.6 |
| Total goods | 99.9 | | | | | | |
| Export growth | | −10.0 | 9.2 | 22.4 | 24.7 | 30.4 | 10.0 |
| Market growth | | 0.5 | 2.9 | 0.2 | −3.9 | 7.8 | 10.6 |
| Export performance[1] | | −10.4 | 6.1 | 22.1 | 29.8 | 20.9 | −0.5 |

1. Calculated as the per cent change in the ratio of Finnish exports over the size of the export market.
*Source:* OECD Secretariat.

## Diagram 2. **COST COMPETITIVENESS**
### Q1 1989 = 100

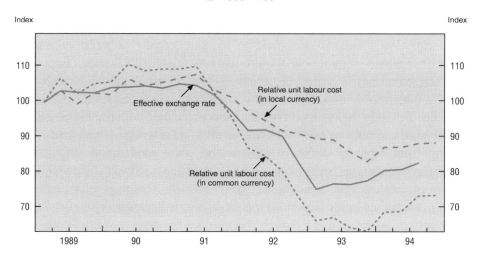

Index                                                                      Index

*Source:* OECD, Secretariat estimates.

6

The reliance of Finnish exports on traditional markets in OECD-Europe has decreased during 1993 and 1994, with their share currently being less than 65 per cent of total exports – down from 73 per cent in 1992 (Diagram 3, Panel A). By contrast, exports to Asia and the United States have been very strong (Table 3) as Finnish manufacturing companies have been particularly competitive in these regions, helped by the strong depreciation of the markka against the US dollar.

Also striking is the strong recovery of exports to former Comecon countries, with Finnish sales to Central and Eastern Europe currently returning to levels that prevailed just before the collapse of trade with this region in 1990/91 (Table 3). This is indicative of the new relationships Finnish exporters are developing in Russia and the Baltic states. In the past, exports to these countries were dominated by large firms operating through the Comecon state agencies. Currently, the move towards market-based management there allows small and medium-sized Finnish firms to transact more directly with local customers, arrange transportation and payments bilaterally, engage in joint ventures and open branch offices on spot.

The export boom since 1991 has been broad based in terms of product categories (Diagram 3, Panel B). Exports of metal and wood products, together constituting around 40 per cent of Finnish external trade, have rapidly recovered from their trough in 1991 and are now at around 150 per cent of their 1988/89 pre-recession level. Paper products, also a very important export category

Table 3. **Destination of Finnish exports**

Percentage changes, nominal

| | 1990 Mk million | 1991 | 1992 | 1993 | 1994[1] |
|---|---|---|---|---|---|
| EFTA | 20 540 | −7.2 | 9.2 | 8.4 | 7.5 |
| EC | 47 514 | 0.1 | 18.3 | 9.5 | 10.7 |
| Other Europe | 14 574 | −71.8 | 12.2 | 54.2 | 33.7 |
| North and South America | 8 669 | −4.7 | 5.8 | 48.2 | – |
| Asia | 7 111 | 18.5 | 11.7 | 51.9 | – |
| Africa | 1 847 | −25.1 | 27.8 | 16.9 | – |
| Other exports of goods | 1 072 | −5.1 | 24.1 | 36.5 | – |
| Total exports of goods | 101 327 | −8.7 | 14.6 | 22.0 | 11.1 |

1. OECD estimate based on first 9 months.
*Source:* Statistics Finland.

Diagram 3. **STRUCTURE OF EXPORTS**

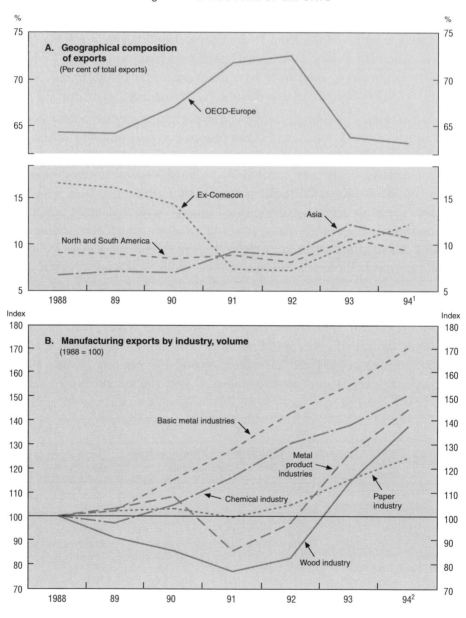

1. Estimates on the basis of first 9 months of 1994.
2. Ministry of Finance estimates.
*Source:* Ministry of Finance; National Board of Customs; OECD, *Foreign Trade Statistics.*

Table 4.  **Export growth by product categories**

1991-1993 [1]

| Product groups and destinations | Food | Wood and wood products | Pulp and paper products | Chemicals and basic metals | Machinery and transport equipment | *of which:* Telecom | Per cent share in total 1993 exports |
|---|---|---|---|---|---|---|---|
| EFTA | 0.7 | 0.6 | 0.4 | 0.9 | 0.2 | 0.5 | 17.0 |
| EC | 0.8 | 0.9 | 0.5 | 1.1 | 0.8 | 0.9 | 46.9 |
| Ex-Comecon [2] | **3.3** | **4.7** | **2.0** | 0.7 | 1.4 | **3.1** | 8.0 |
| Japan | – | – | **2.0** | 1.5 | 0.5 | 0.5 | 1.6 |
| Other Asia [3] | – | – | **4.4** | 1.3 | **2.7** | 1.5 | 5.2 |
| United States | – | – | **5.2** | **2.0** | 1.1 | **2.5** | 7.8 |
| Per cent share in total 1993 exports | 2.8 | 7.5 | 27.0 | 15.3 | 31.5 | 5.2 | |

1.  The table shows the growth in exports per product group to each region, as a ratio to overall export growth, in current markka prices. A number less than one therefore indicates below average export growth, and *vice versa*. Exports growth exceeding twice the average is indicated by a bolded number. A dash indicates that exports to the region or country were insignificant in 1991.
2.  (Ex-)USSR, Poland, Hungary. For 1933, ex-USSR comprises Russia and Estonia.
3.  China, Hong Kong, Korea, Thailand, Indonesia.
*Source:* National Board of Customs, Finland and OECD Secretariat.

(around 25 per cent of total exports), increased rapidly as well, although their upswing has been somewhat less spectacular. The geographical breakdown of exports for each product category (Table 4) shows that exports of wood and paper have been strong in all markets outside Europe. Another significant development is the rapid growth in exports of telecom products to both the ex-Comecon countries and the United States.

## Still sluggish private demand

### *Progress in balance sheet consolidation*

One of the main factors behind the weakness of domestic demand in recent years has been the attempts by households and firms to reduce their debt burdens which, by the early 1990s, had risen to levels far above historical averages (Diagram 4). As discussed in previous surveys, debt accumulation by the private sector was essentially the result of the interaction, in the 1980s, of financial deregulation and tax incentives for debt-financed investment. Debt levels

Diagram 4.  **PROGRESS IN FINANCIAL CONSOLIDATION**

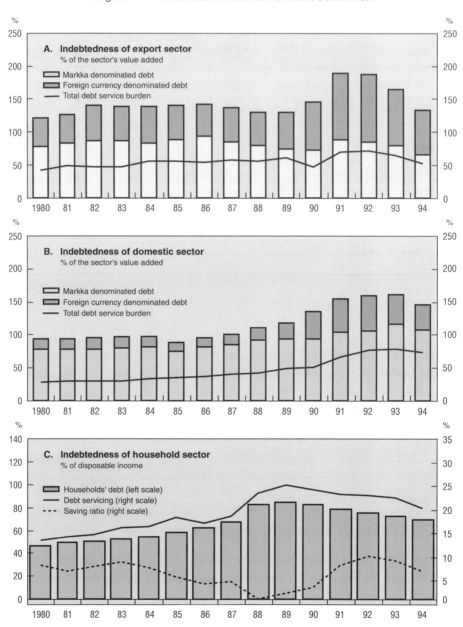

Source:  Bank of Finland.

increased further in the aftermath of the currency depreciation in 1991-92, as this boosted the markka value of corporate loans denominated in foreign currency. Incentives to reduce debt were strengthened by the tightening of monetary policy in the early 1990s and by tax reforms, both of which increased the cost of debt service considerably.

Financial consolidation in the private sector has been greatly facilitated by the easing of monetary conditions over 1993-94 (see Part II), which has reduced debt interest payments by large amounts, and by the emerging recovery. In the export manufacturing industries, the rapid expansion of output since the devaluation in 1991 has enhanced the ability of firms to repay debt. As a result, the debt ratio in manufacturing is at present estimated to have returned to the levels that prevailed in the mid-1980s. The household sector has also achieved a considerable reduction in its debt ratio since 1990, but much less progress has been made in the domestic-oriented business sector, which is still facing a debt ratio that is 50 per cent higher than the historical average. This largely results from the dramatic fall in value added in this sector, which occurred between 1990 and early 1994.

## Household demand

The volume of private consumption fell in 1993 for the fourth successive year (Diagram 5, Panel A). This decline was broadly proportional to the reduction in real disposable income (Table 5), as the household saving ratio finally stabilised in 1993 after the increases recorded in previous years (Diagram 4, Panel C). Though cushioned by the lower debt servicing costs and tax refunds (see Part II), real disposable income declined by a further 4 per cent in 1993. This reflected the continued rise in unemployment and the impact of the 1993 freeze in contractual wages.

Real growth in private consumption turned positive in late 1993, to reach a 3$^{1}/_{2}$ per cent annual rate (seasonally-adjusted) in the first half of 1994. The turnaround has been most pronounced for household expenditure on consumer durables (Diagram 5, Panels B and C). One illustration of this is the gradual increase in the number of car registrations, with car purchases in June 1994 up by 25 per cent on a year-on-year basis.[1] These developments mirror a gradual improvement in consumer confidence, which – according to most recent surveys – has now returned to levels registered in 1987/88 (Diagram 5, Panel A).

11

Diagram 5. **HOUSEHOLD SPENDING**

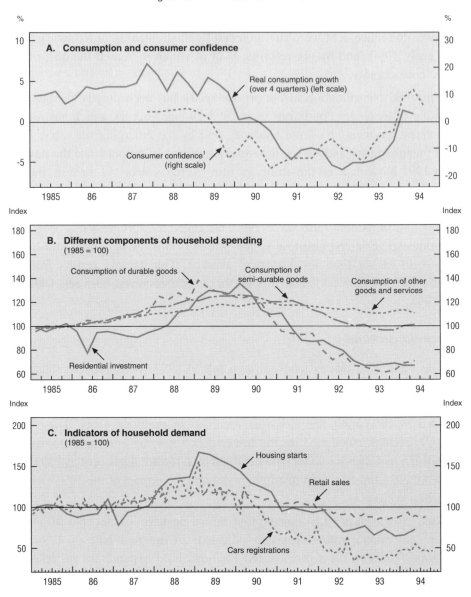

1. The indicator reflects consumer perception of economic developments for the past 12 and next 12 months and whether present conditions are conducive to larger purchases.
*Source:* OECD, *Quartely National Accounts, Main Economic Indicators.*

12

Table 5. **Household appropriation account**

Percentage changes, volume (1990 prices)

| | 1990 current prices Mk billion | 1991 | 1992 | 1993 | 1994 [1] |
|---|---|---|---|---|---|
| Real disposable income | 271.0 | 1.1 | –2.9 | –4.4 | –2.6 |
| Contributions from: | | | | | |
| Wages | 300.8 | –4.6 | –7.5 | –7.7 | –0.2 |
| Entrepreneurial and property income | 78.2 | –1.6 | –0.3 | –1.9 | 1.5 |
| Net transfers to households | 101.6 | 4.3 | 2.2 | 1.0 | –1.1 |
| Interest on consumer debt [2] | 28.9 | 0 | 0.3 | 2.3 | 1.0 |
| Direct taxes [2] | 82.5 | 3.1 | 2.4 | 2.0 | –3.9 [3] |
| Real consumption expenditure | 269.7 | –3.6 | –4.9 | –4.1 | –0.5 |
| Saving ratio, in level [4] | 0.4 | 5.1 | 7.0 | 6.6 | 4.2 |

1. *Economic Outlook*, No. 56.
2. A positive number indicates that real interest payments or real direct taxes have fallen.
3. Direct tax payments for 1994 are heavily affected by a postponement of tax refunds to 1995, see Part II.
4. Ratio of household saving to disposable household income (non-profit institutions have been included in the household sector).
*Source:* OECD Secretariat.

The rebound in consumption is essentially underpinned by resumed growth in real incomes (including household entrepreneurial income) and a further fall in debt servicing costs. Nonetheless, for 1994 as a whole real household income may register a decrease, due to the postponement of tax refunds from December 1994 to early 1995 (see Part II) (Table 5).

While there is still no evidence of a sustained increase in housing starts and residential investment, these have nonetheless stopped declining (Diagram 5, Panels B and C). The number of dwellings traded started to grow in the first months of 1993, and reached more or less normal levels towards the end of that year. As a result, the stock of unsold new dwellings has declined considerably. Housing prices bottomed in early 1993 and, by the second quarter of 1994, had registered an 8 per cent increase on a year-on-year basis before falling back somewhat late in the summer. Price rises have been particularly strong in the Helsinki region.

Diagram 6.  **BUSINESS INVESTMENT**

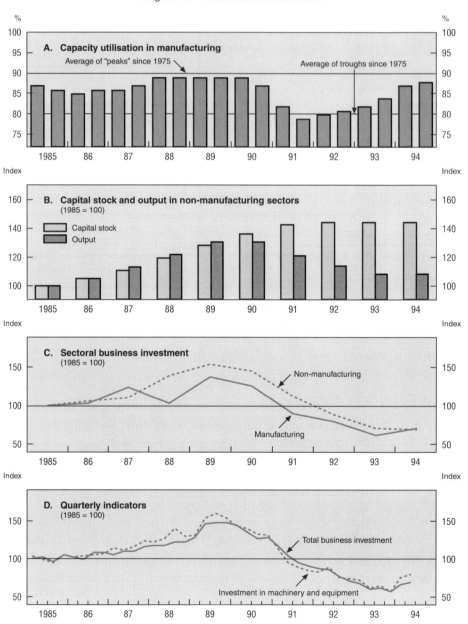

*Source:* Bank of Finland;  OECD, *National Accounts,* Secretariat estimates.

14

*Business investment*

Capital formation in the business sector remained weak in 1993 (Table 1). Two factors appear to have contributed to this development. On the one hand, relatively high, though declining, real interest rates prompted companies to postpone investment projects. On the other hand, firms in the non-manufacturing sector continued to experience large amounts of excess capacity, as the result of the recession (Diagram 6, Panel B). According to Bank of Finland estimates, manufacturing investment started to recover in 1994, spurred by capacity utilisation approaching historical peak levels (Diagram 6, Panel A). Easier monetary conditions and enhanced corporate profitability also played a role in this regard. Investment in machinery and equipment has been particularly strong in the first half of 1994, with growth rates possibly exceeding 100 per cent. Overall, however, business investment still remains relatively low by historical standards.

## High but declining unemployment

With economic activity gradually edging up, total employment stabilised in the winter of 1993/94 and, by September 1994, had grown in seasonally adjusted terms by 1.6 per cent from its level a year earlier (Diagram 7, Panel A). As the labour force continued to decline, albeit at a slower pace, the unemployment rate peaked in early 1994 at about 19.2 per cent, before falling to 18.2 per cent by September; the vacancy rate also began to rise from its historically low levels in 1993 (Diagram 7, Panel B). The largest absolute sectoral decline in employment has been in the service sector where, in June 1994, employment was 240 000 below its 1990 peak. More striking is the fact that the manufacturing sector, which has experienced rapid growth since its trough in 1991, had downsized its work force by 18 per cent by mid-1994. This reflects the significant productivity gains achieved in this sector.

## Low inflation

Due to the large slack in the labour market, wage pressures continued to be moderate during 1993. Hourly earnings rose by only 0.8 per cent, half the rate recorded in 1992, with somewhat larger increases in the manufacturing sector

Diagram 7. **THE LABOUR MARKET**

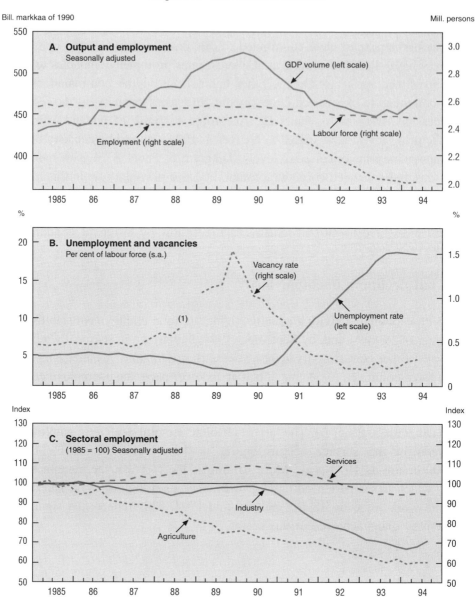

Bill. markkaa of 1990

**A. Output and employment**
Seasonally adjusted

GDP volume (left scale)

Employment (right scale)

Labour force (right scale)

Mill. persons

**B. Unemployment and vacancies**
Per cent of labour force (s.a.)

Vacancy rate
(right scale)

Unemployment rate
(left scale)

(1)

**C. Sectoral employment**
(1985 = 100) Seasonally adjusted

Services

Industry

Agriculture

Index

1. Break in 1988 due to a change of legislation forcing firms to declare vacant jobs to employment offices.
*Source: OECD, National Accounts, Main Economic Indicators.*

16

(Table 6). As was also the case in 1992, increases in hourly earnings in 1993 were almost exclusively due to wage drift; negotiated hourly wages remained unchanged due to a twelve-month wage freeze effective up to October. Even though rising employers' contributions to the unemployment insurance funds led to increases in labour costs exceeding those in gross earnings, unit labour costs remained on their downward trend owing to continued rapid productivity growth. With pay rise settlements in manufacturing averaging 3 per cent for the twelve months starting October 1993, wage growth has been accelerating in 1994. Indeed, hourly earnings in manufacturing have risen by some 4¾ per cent from the second quarter of 1993 to the second quarter of 1994. As a result, while wage growth in the non-manufacturing sector has remained subdued, hourly earnings growth for the economy as a whole reached 2.0 per cent in the second quarter of 1994 compared with the same period a year earlier. This is about three times the rate recorded in 1993.

Table 6. **Prices, wages and costs**

Percentage changes

|  | 1991 | 1992 | 1993 | 1994[1] |
|---|---|---|---|---|
| **Consumer prices** | 4.1 | 2.6 | 2.2 | 1.2 |
| Contribution from: |  |  |  |  |
| Indirect taxes net of subsidies | 1.6 | 1.4 | 1.5 | 0.7 |
| Housing costs and interest rates | 0.1 | −0.3 | −1.0 | −0.3 |
| Import prices | 0.1 | 0.9 | 1.1 | 0.0 |
| Labour costs | 3.6 | −1.2 | −1.4 | −1.0 |
| Profit margins and capital costs | −1.3 | 1.8 | 2.0 | 1.8 |
| **Hourly labour and wage costs** |  |  |  |  |
| Whole economy |  |  |  |  |
| Average earnings | 6.4 | 1.9 | 0.8 | 2.0[3] |
| Total labour costs | 7.0 | 1.8 | 2.9 | − |
| Unit labour costs[2] | 7.8 | −2.5 | −3.0 | − |
| Manufacturing |  |  |  |  |
| Average earnings | 6.2 | 2.1 | 1.5 | 4.8[3] |
| Total labour costs | 5.8 | 4.4 | 4.2 | − |
| Unit labour costs[2] | 5.9 | −8.0 | −6.6 | − |

1. Estimate made in September 1994 by Bank of Finland, for the whole year of 1994.
2. Labour costs per unit of output (defined in terms of value added in constant prices).
3. Change from third quarter 1993 to same quarter 1994.
*Source:* Bank of Finland.

Diagram 8.  **PRICE DEVELOPMENTS**

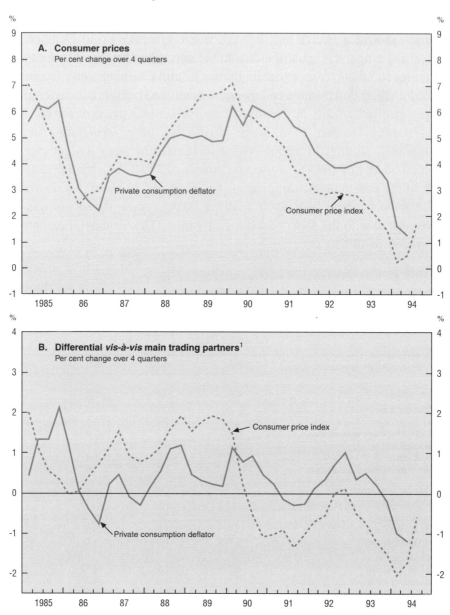

1.  Finland minus partners.
*Source:* OECD, *Main Economic Indicators, Quarterly National Accounts*, Secretariat estimates.

18

Helped by continued weak labour costs and, more recently, stable import prices due to the appreciation of the markka since early 1993, inflation pressure has remained weak in 1993 and 1994. The increase in the consumer price index (CPI) was practically zero by early 1994, before edging up, due the replacement of the turnover tax by a value-added tax on services in June (Diagram 8, Panel A).[2] However, gauged by the private consumption deflator, the inflation performance has been somewhat less favourable – both in absolute terms and in terms of inflation differentials *vis-à-vis* trading partners (Diagram 8, Panel B). This is explained by the fact that the private consumption deflator does not capture the impact of the fall in housing prices and (until recently) of the drop in short-term interest rates on the cost of living for Finnish households. Indeed, when increases in the CPI in 1993 and 1994 are separated into their principal components, housing costs and the costs of debt servicing, together with labour costs, show a significantly negative contribution (Table 6). At the same time, positive effects came from the recovery in profit margins as well as from the increase in *net* indirect taxes, reflecting cuts in subsidy programmes in the 1993 Budget and, as noted, the 1994 reform of indirect taxation.

## Improved external position

Strong exports and weak imports have led to a gradual improvement in the merchandise trade balance, to a surplus of 9 per cent of GDP in the first half of 1994 (Diagram 9, Panel A). Moreover, after four years of steady deterioration in the terms of trade – totalling 14 per cent from 1989 to 1993 – these reversed in the first half of 1994, partly reflecting the worldwide price recovery of forestry products, which, as noted, are dominant in Finnish exports. With domestic demand recovering, import growth has in 1994 proved substantially faster than the increase in exports. Nevertheless, for 1994 as a whole, the trade surplus is estimated to reach 10 per cent of GDP. The deficit in the service balance has also narrowed, mainly reflecting a reduction in net expenditure on tourism. As a result, after turning to approximate balance by the end of 1993, the current account of the balance of payments showed a surplus of 1½ per cent of GDP in the first half of 1994 (Diagram 9, Panel A). This improvement has taken place in spite of increases in the servicing cost of foreign debt, associated with the earlier depreciation of the markka. With the exchange rate appreciating since early 1993

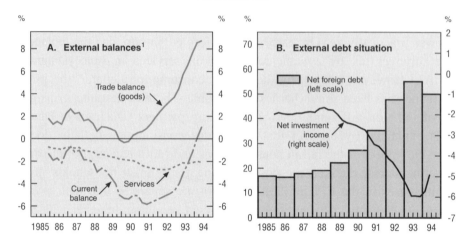

Diagram 9. **THE EXTERNAL POSITION**
Per cent of GDP

1. 4 quarters moving average.
*Source:* OECD.

and the current account surplus continuing to increase, net foreign debt is falling while net investment income remains roughly constant as a percentage of GDP (Diagram 9, Panel B).

## Short-term outlook

The recovery is projected to gather momentum over the projection period and to become more broadly based. With the employment outlook improving and households' financial consolidation coming to an end, an upswing in private consumption is projected for 1995 and 1996, at a pace of around 5 per cent (Table 7). Even stronger growth is expected for private sector investment volumes, in particular in manufacturing where these are presently low in view of output projections and the already high rates of capacity utilisation. Indeed, a recent business survey suggests that the manufacturing sector could attain double-digit growth rates of investment in both 1994 and 1995. The strong trade performance of recent years is projected to level off, as no further gains in

Table 7. **Short-term projections**

Percentage changes, volume (1990 prices)

| | 1993 current prices Mk billion | 1994 | 1995 | 1996 |
|---|---|---|---|---|
| Private consumption | 237.6 | 0.1 | 5.0 | 5.0 |
| Government consumption | 102.9 | –3.1 | –1.5 | –1.0 |
| Gross fixed capital formation | 74.7 | 6.9 | 12.9 | 9.9 |
| *of which:* | | | | |
| Public sector | 14.4 | –8.7 | –1.5 | 0.5 |
| Business sector | 38.4 | 15.1 | 17.7 | 12.7 |
| Residential | 21.9 | 2.6 | 12.0 | 8.9 |
| Final domestic demand | 415.2 | 0.5 | 4.9 | 4.7 |
| Stockbuilding [1] | 2.4 | 0.6 | 0.4 | 0.0 |
| Total domestic demand | 412.8 | 1.2 | 5.4 | 4.6 |
| Exports of goods and services | 142.3 | 10.8 | 7.0 | 5.1 |
| Imports of goods and services | 113.4 | 6.0 | 9.1 | 7.4 |
| Foreign balance [1] | 28.9 | 1.9 | 0.0 | –0.2 |
| GDP | 452.4 | 3.5 | 4.8 | 3.9 |
| Household saving ratio [2] | | 4.0 | 7.1 | 4.2 |
| Private consumption deflator | | 1.7 | 2.1 | 2.5 |
| GDP deflator | | 1.7 | 2.1 | 2.9 |
| Unit labour cost in manufacturing | | –0.8 | 1.3 | 1.6 |
| Net lending of general government | | | | |
| Per cent of GDP | | –4.7 | –5.1 | –3.9 |
| Current account | | | | |
| Per cent of GDP | | 2.4 | 2.8 | 2.9 |
| US$ billion | | 2.1 | 3.0 | 3.3 |
| Unemployment rate | | 18.3 | 16.3 | 14.6 |

1. Contribution to growth of GDP, includes statistical discrepancy.
2. Households and non-profit institutions, percent of disposable income.
*Source:* OECD Secretariat.

international cost competitiveness are expected and capacity constraints in manufacturing industries may increase. With imports responding to the revival of domestic demand, net foreign trade should not contribute to output growth.

Overall, real GDP growth, which is estimated to have reached 3½ per cent in 1994, should accelerate to around 4½ per cent on average in the following two years. Given a projected slowing in productivity gains, employment should

21

stabilise in 1994 and may increase by roughly $2^{1}/_{2}$ to 3 per cent annually in 1995 and 1996. With a projected continued weak growth of the labour force, the unemployment rate could fall to a level close to 14 per cent by the end of 1996. Inflation pressures are expected to remain modest over the projection period, due to the continued slack in the sheltered non-manufacturing sectors. The increase in consumer prices associated with the expected rise in housing costs and the change in the indirect taxation regime will be offset by the lower food prices resulting from EU-membership. Finally, following an estimated increase to about 2 per cent of GDP in 1994, some modest further rise in the current account surplus is expected, mainly reflecting a slight improvement in the terms of trade and a narrowing of the investment income deficit due to the reduced servicing cost of foreign debt.

These projections are based upon the following main assumptions:

- a sustained economic expansion in the OECD area, leading to Finnish export market growth of $7^{1}/_{2}$ per cent in 1995 and 1996;
- a reduction in public expenditure in line with the 1995 Budget proposal, implying a further fall in general government consumption and investment;
- a narrowing of long-term interest differentials with German rates, reflecting continued low inflation pressure. On the other hand, short-term rates are assumed to firm somewhat towards the end of the projection period in line with developments in Germany;
- a stabilisation of the exchange rate at its November 1994 level.

The main uncertainty attached to these projections is whether the revival of domestic demand will be strong enough to keep economic growth sustained. There is concern in particular, that the recent increases in long-term interest rates, which have been more pronounced in Finland than in many other OECD countries (see below in Part II), hurt the nascent recovery of investment. Another uncertainty relates to wage and price developments. Increased employment opportunities in the exporting industries may be reflected in a rebound of wage growth. As this could spill over to the rest of the economy due to collective wage bargaining, there is a risk that domestic inflation may prove stronger than projected.

# II. Economic policies

## Overview

After the exceptional shocks which adversely affected the economy in the early 1990s, both fiscal and monetary policies have aimed at restoring confidence in financial markets while creating the conditions for a non-inflationary recovery. On the fiscal side, austerity measures have been implemented to reduce growing budget deficits and public debt, mainly through substantial reductions in government investment and consumption. Monetary policy has focused on keeping inflation low in order to regain credibility, thereby allowing a progressive easing of interest rates to support activity while preserving the gains in competitiveness achieved in the period 1991 to 1993. At the same time, an important support scheme has been put in place to ensure the stability of the financial system, following the sharp deterioration of banks' balance sheets. This has been supplemented by some restructuring of the banking industry and a strengthening of bank supervision. Emphasis on structural reform has also been maintained to improve economic efficiency and prepare the grounds for full participation in the European integration process. The present chapter reviews these macroeconomic and structural policy developments, with particular attention to the initiatives taken over the last eighteen months or so.

## The fiscal stance

### Budgetary developments in 1993 and 1994

The deterioration in the general government financial position registered in 1992 continued into 1993, with the deficit increasing to 7.1 per cent of GDP – 1.2 percentage points above the 1992 level. Excluding the social security surplus the 1993 deficit would have exceeded 10 per cent of GDP.[3] This deterioration occurred despite new austerity measures to curb spending, notably public consumption (wages), investment and subsidies (Table 8). Since new capital injections in the banking sector were relatively small in 1993 (see below), the public sector borrowing requirement increased by roughly the same amount as the general government deficit.

The surge in the 1993 deficit was mainly attributable to a fall in direct tax revenues, a sharp rise in transfers to households and increased debt servicing costs (Table 8). The decline in tax receipts reflected a shrinking of the tax base due to the prolonged recession, as well as the impact of two tax refunds with

Table 8.  **General government budget**

Mk billion, change from previous year

|  | 1991 | 1992 | 1993 | 1994 | Cumulated 1991-1994 |
|---|---|---|---|---|---|
| **Current receipts** | **−4.1** | **−3.8** | **−0.8** | **14.8** | **6.1** |
| *of which:* | | | | | |
| Direct tax households | −4.2 | −3.9 | −3.2 | 12.1 | 0.9 |
| Direct tax business | −0.4 | −1.9 | −4.2 | −0.2 | −6.8 |
| Indirect tax | −3.3 | −3.1 | −0.3 | −1.4 | −8.1 |
| Social security contributions | 0.9 | 2.5 | 5.8 | 4.9 | 14.1 |
| Other[1] | 2.9 | 2.0 | 1.1 | −0.7 | 6.0 |
| **Current expenditure** | **30.9** | **15.4** | **15.5** | **5.2** | **67.0** |
| *of which:* | | | | | |
| Consumption | 10.2 | −0.2 | −5.6 | −4.3 | 0.1 |
| Subsidies | 2.4 | −0.6 | −0.7 | −0.7 | 0.4 |
| Unemployment benefits | 6.8 | 9.7 | 5.6 | 1.4 | 23.5 |
| Pensions | 5.9 | 5.6 | 9.1 | 2.3 | 15.8 |
| Other current transfers | 3.6 | −2.0 | 4.5 | 1.6 | 7.7 |
| Interest | 2.1 | 3.0 | 9.5 | 4.9 | 19.4 |
| **Net capital expenditure**[2] | **0.0** | **−3.0** | **−2.5** | **−0.2** | **−5.7** |
| **Net lending** | **−35.0** | **−16.2** | **−13.8** | **9.8** | **−55.2** |
| | Per cent of GDP | | | | |
| Revenues | 52.5 | 53.4 | 53.8 | 54.1 | – |
| Expenditure | 54.5 | 59.3 | 60.9 | 58.0 | – |
| Net lending | −1.5 | −5.9 | −7.1 | −4.7 | – |

1.   Other transfers and property incomes.
2.   Investment, depreciation and capital transfers.
*Source:* Ministry of Finance.

respect to both 1991 and 1992 income. The recession also triggered an increase in social security transfers, in particular unemployment and early retirement benefits. The rapid accumulation of public debt in 1992, in the wake of the banking crisis, is the main factor behind the increase in interest payments which, with the bulk of debt being issued by the state, primarily weighs upon the central government budget. This, together with the fact that the cuts in public consumption mainly fell upon the local government budget, explains the large increase in the central government deficit from 7.6 per cent of GDP in 1992 to 10 per cent of GDP in 1993. Indeed, the planned central government deficit for 1993 was overshot by almost Mk 20 billion (around 4 per cent of GDP, Table 9).

Table 9. **Initial budget proposals and outcomes**

Mk billion

| | 1991 | 1992 | 1993 | | 1994 | | 1995 |
| | Outcome | | Proposed | Outcome | Proposed | Estimated outcome | Proposed |
|---|---|---|---|---|---|---|---|
| **Central government** | | | | | | | |
| Revenue | 132.1 | 125.8 | 120 | 118.9 | 125 | 125.0 | 134 |
| Expenditure | 153.8 | 162.2 | 155 | 172.4 | 177 | 176.5 | 187 |
| Balance | −21.7 | −36.4 | −35 | −53.5 | −52 | −51.5 | −53 |
| **Social Security** | | | | | | | |
| Revenue | 95.6 | 102.7 | 120 | 127.3 | 137 | 139.6 | 147 |
| Expenditure | 76.6 | 90.4 | 100 | 108.6 | 116 | 118.8 | 121 |
| Balance | 19.0 | 12.3 | 18 | 18.7 | 21 | 20.8 | 25 |
| **Local Government** | | | | | | | |
| Revenue | 92.0 | 91.4 | 90 | 92.2 | 93 | 96.9 | 92 |
| Expenditure | 96.3 | 95.2 | 93 | 92.9 | 92 | 89.7 | 91 |
| Balance | −4.3 | −3.8 | −3 | −0.7 | 1 | 7.2 | 1 |
| *Memorandum items:* | | | | | | | |
| General government balance (% of GDP) | −1.5 | −5.9 | −5.1 | −7.1 | −6.2 | −4.7 | −5 |
| Projections underlying the budget estimates | | | | | | | |
| GDP growth | −7.1 | −3.6 | 2½ | −2.0 | 1 | 3½ | 4½ |
| Unemployment rate | 7.6 | 13.1 | 13 | 17.9 | 19 | 18½ | 16½ |

*Source:* Ministry of Finance.

The Budget proposal for 1994 envisaged a stabilisation of the central government deficit at its 1993 level. Helped by the "tax bonus" resulting from the stronger-than-expected recovery, and despite three supplementary budgets in March, June and October adding Mk 6.4 billion to expenditure, this deficit target is expected to be reached (Table 9). Public consumption and investment are still on a downward trend, the latter despite a front loading of infrastructure projects implied by the March supplementary budget. Income transfers should stabilise, partly due to cuts in grants to the local government. By contrast, interest payments on public debt continue to grow rapidly. On the revenue side, tax proceeds have been boosted by the postponement of tax refunds to 1995. With the local government surplus rising in 1994, primarily reflecting the delay in tax refunds, and the social security surplus widening as a result of a modest fall in unemployment, the general government deficit is estimated to decline substantially from 7.1 per cent of GDP in 1993 to 4.7 per cent in 1994 – a better outcome than foreseen in the 1994 Budget proposal.

## The 1995 Budget

The Budget proposal for 1995, which was presented to Parliament in September 1994, is dominated by the impact of the EU accession on public finance. As a result of EU membership, central government expenditure is projected to increase by Mk 14 billion, *i.e.* around 3 per cent of GDP, in 1995. This largely reflects rising income support to farmers to compensate for an expected reduction of Finnish agricultural prices, and a general contribution to the EU budget. As the central government will also receive transfers from the EU (*e.g.* through the structural adjustment fund), the net impact of EU membership on the 1995 central government budget deficit may be around 2 per cent of GDP. Consequently, given the two tax refunds planned in 1995 (with respect to 1993 and 1994 income), and despite stronger economic activity, the central government deficit is expected only to stabilise at around Mk 50 billion, or 10 per cent of GDP. Since, at the same time, the surplus of local governments is envisaged to fall substantially (Table 9), mainly due to refunds of local taxes, the general government deficit is officially projected to increase to 5 per cent of GDP in 1995.

Adjusted for budgetary cost of EU membership and the one-off impact of tax refunds, the 1995 general government deficit would be around $3\frac{1}{2}$ per cent of GDP lower than officially expected. Likewise, the 1993 deficit would be reduced

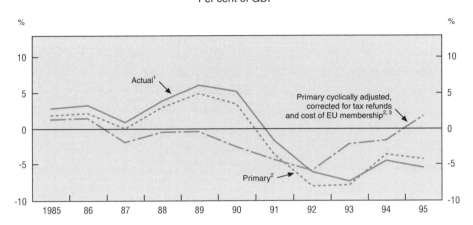

Diagram 10. **GENERAL GOVERNMENT BALANCES**
Per cent of GDP

1. Net lending.
2. Net lending excluding net interest receipts.
3. As per cent of potential GDP.
*Source:* OECD, Secretariat estimates.

by 1½ per cent of GDP if corrected for the tax refunds implemented that year. Thus, the "underlying" development of budget deficits seems to suggest a tighter orientation of fiscal policy since 1993. This is corroborated by the Secretariat's fiscal indicators, which for the period 1992 to 1995 as a whole, show a decline in the cyclically-adjusted primary deficit (*i.e.* net of debt interest payments) after correction for tax refunds and EU accession – see Diagram 10. Although the scope of such indicators is limited in the case of Finland, given the large swings in output experienced by the country since the early 1990s excluding the special factors signalled above, significant progress in restoring control over government finance has been accomplished in recent years.

## *The debt constraint*

Gross public debt is officially projected to reach 72½ per cent of GDP by the end of 1994, up from 15 per cent in the late 1980s (Diagram 11). This is a more rapid deterioration of the debt position than in most other OECD economies. Such evolution is of even more concern when the impact of the ageing

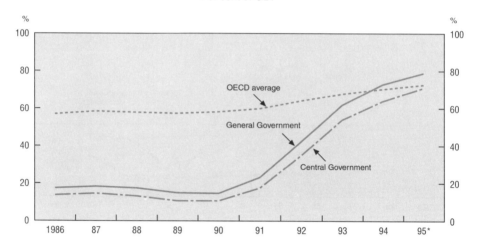

Diagram 11. **GROSS PUBLIC DEBT**
Per cent of GDP

* Projection by the Ministry of Finance.
*Source:* Ministry of Finance and Statistics Finland.

population on future welfare expenditure is taken into account. As discussed in detail in Part III, pension payments will start rapidly increasing towards the end of this decade, when the post-war "baby-boom" generation reaches the age of possible early retirement. This will generate substantial pressure on government finances, as the public pension schemes are currently heavily underfunded. Indeed, projected future entitlements by far exceed the financial assets accumulated by the schemes so far.[4] Even when taking into account future contributions to the schemes, by both employers and employees, the underfunding of the pension system would still look high in Finland, comparable to other OECD countries (Table 10).

In such circumstances, as real long-term interest rates are presently significantly above current and projected growth rates, the general government primary balance should be in surplus in order to stabilise the debt/GDP ratio at its present level. This being not yet the case (Diagram 10), further fiscal consolidation will thus be needed. As the prevailing tax pressure in the Finnish economy is already relatively high (53 per cent of GDP), this might preferably take the form of

Table 10. **Contingent liabilities[1] of the public pension schemes**

1990, per cent of GDP

| | Currently retired (a) | Current workforce (b) | Future workforce[2] (c) | Total contingent liabilities (a + b + c) | Memorandum item: Existing assets |
|---|---|---|---|---|---|
| **Finland** | **123** | **133** | **−77** | **179** | **38** |
| United States | 42 | 49 | −14 | 77 | 23 |
| Japan | 51 | 122 | 8 | 181 | 18 |
| Germany | 55 | 94 | −2 | 147 | − |
| France | 77 | 123 | −7 | 193 | − |
| Italy | 94 | 143 | −11 | 226 | − |
| United Kingdom | 58 | 94 | 1 | 153 | − |
| Canada | 42 | 52 | 22 | 116 | 8 |

1.  Net present value of future flows of pension benefits and pension contributions. The estimates are subject to large margins of error, and highly sensitive to changes in assumptions with respect to future benefit levels.
2.  Children living in 1990.
*Source:* Van den Noord, P. and Herd, R., "Pension liabilities in the seven major economies", *OECD Working paper 142*, December 1993; and submission by VATT, Government Institute for Economic Research, Helsinki.

additional spending restraint, beyond the official objective of limiting the volume of central government expenditure (disregarding support to the banking sector and the budgetary cost of EU membership) to its 1991 level by 1995.

# Monetary management

## *Policy objectives*

Following the decision to let the markka float in September 1992, the thrust of Finnish monetary policy has been to reduce interest rates in order to support an economy in deep recession while, at the same time, restoring confidence in the currency and preserving price stability. Regaining credibility was regarded as the key to achieve these goals. To this end, the central bank announced, in February 1993, an explicit inflation target which was subsequently endorsed by the Government. The objective was to stabilise the underlying rate of inflation – measured by the consumer price index excluding indirect taxes, subsidies and housing capital costs – at 2 per cent from 1995 onwards (see Box 1 for more details). However, to take account of the repercussions of the currency deprecia-tion, no target was announced for the interim period.

## Box 1. **The Finnish indicator of underlying inflation**

Similarly to other countries where central banks pursue inflation objectives, the impact of changes in indirect taxes is excluded from the targeted Indicator of Underlying Inflation (IUI) in Finland. As in the United Kingdom and New Zealand, the effects of changes in mortgage costs are also removed. The calculation of the indicator is carried out by Statistics Finland, making it free of political interferences.* The measurement was modified in 1992 in the context of a change in agricultural subsidies.

Diagram 12 plots three measures of inflation (the contents of which are documented in the table below): the standard consumer price index (CPI), the private consumption deflator excluding the effects of indirect taxes and subsidies (NPI) and the IUI. The Diagram shows that the CPI has been more erratic than either the NPI and IUI since early 1993, and has tended to understate inflationary pressures relative to IUI. However, the IUI and the NPI are less widely used than the CPI, their advantages being most apparent under circumstances such as the substantial easing of monetary policy in 1993. In general, however, as evidenced by developments in the period 1991-92, these indicators do not provide inflation signals significantly different from the CPI.

* A full documentation is provided in "Net Price Index and Tax Rate Index 1990 = 100", Lehtinen, Ilkka, Statistics Finland, 1994.

| | The Indicator of Underlying Inflation in Finland | |
| --- | --- | --- |
| | Level in Mk billion[1] | Weights of components of consumption[1] |
| **Base for CPI index:** | | |
| Total household consumption expenditure | 241 | 100 |
| Net indirect taxes | 55 | 23 |
| of which: | | |
| Gross indirect taxes | 66 | 27 |
| Subsidies | –11 | –4 |
| **Base for Net Price Index:** | | |
| Household consumption minus net indirect taxes | 186 | 77 |
| Capital cost of owner-occupied housing | 24 | 10 |
| **Base for Indicator of Underlying Inflation** | | |
| Household consumption minus net indirect taxes | | |
| and capital costs of owner-occupied housing | 161 | 67 |

1. Weights of the different components are derived from 1990 input-output tables.
*Source:* Lehtinen, Ilkka, "Net Price Index and Tax Rate Index 1990 = 100", Statistics Finland 1994.

Judged by price developments up to the fall of 1994, it seems likely that the target will be achieved in 1995. Indeed, after remaining in the range of 2 to 3 per cent in 1993, the indicator of underlying inflation declined to 1.3 per cent in September 1994 (Diagram 12). Such an impressive inflation performance – particularly in view of the significant depreciation of the currency – should be seen, however, against the weak domestic conditions prevailing since the adoption of the target. Thus, it is not clear to what extent the new formulation of monetary policy has really contributed to contain inflation expectations. The fact is, as discussed below, that long-term interest rates remain high relative to inflation and have been rising recently, with concerns about public finances probably playing a significant role. This would seem to suggest that policy credibility is not yet fully established, so that it will be necessary to wait to see how prices develop during the emerging upswing before assessing progress in this regard.

Some institutional changes suggested by a recent draft law[5] might help strengthen credibility, in particular a more binding mandate for the Bank of Finland to maintain price stability.[6] This would help ensure that policy remains

Diagram 12. **INFLATION PERFORMANCE**
Per cent change over 12 months

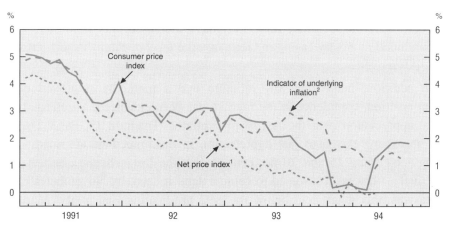

1. Consumer price index, net of indirect taxes and subsidies.
2. Net price index, adjusted for housing capital costs.
*Source:* Statistics Finland; OECD, *Main Economic Indicators.*

consistent with inflation objectives over time. Shifting the decisions on changes in official interest rates from the Parliamentary Central Bank Supervisory Committee to the Board of the Bank of Finland – another reform suggested by the Law proposal – would also contribute to enhance the effectiveness of monetary policy. In addition, as short-run deviations from the official inflation objective are unavoidable, the possible loss of credibility such deviations might entail could be limited through the announcement of a narrow range of permissible inflation rates, of for example, 1 to 3 per cent. However, while facilitating the achievement of the target, such an approach might raise suspicions that the monetary authorities in fact aim at an inflation rate at the upper end of the range. In any event, as noted, the ability of the authorities to improve the inflation performance of the Finnish economy is yet to be tested, now that economic activity is gathering strength and wage pressures are gradually building up.

### Interest rate developments and exchange rate behaviour

Continuing weak economic activity and success in keeping price and wage inflation under control has left room for a substantial reduction of short-term interest rates. Following the floating of the currency, the three-month money market rate was gradually reduced from $16^{1}/_{2}$ per cent in September 1992 to $4^{3}/_{4}$ per cent in February/March 1994 (Diagram 13, Panel A). By mid-1993, short-term differentials with German rates had been eliminated, and they turned negative in early 1994. Since then, they have increased only modestly, so that with continued monetary easing in Germany, the *level* of Finnish short-term rates has hardly moved.

In addition, helped by low inflation and a markedly improved current account position, confidence in the markka has been enhanced, as reflected in its gradual appreciation over the last twelve months (Diagram 13, Panel B). As a result, the sharp exchange rate depreciation in the immediate aftermath of the floating – by some 25 and 20 per cent against the Deutschemark and the Ecu, respectively – has been reversed to some extent. Indeed, by November 1994 the markka was only 4 per cent below its 1992 pre-floating Ecu parity. Moreover, interventions in the currency market by the Bank of Finland have mainly aimed to smooth exchange rate volatility: support was given when the markka fell in early 1993, but foreign currency was bought to prevent a too rapid appreciation in December 1993 and January 1994 (Diagram 14, Panel A). The sharp increase

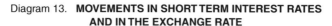

Diagram 13. **MOVEMENTS IN SHORT TERM INTEREST RATES AND IN THE EXCHANGE RATE**

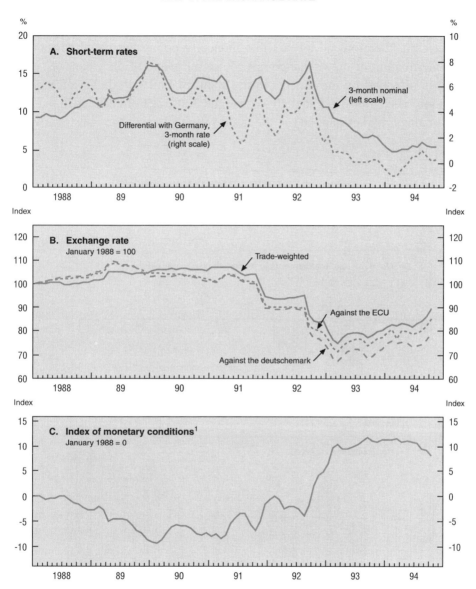

A. Short-term rates

3-month nominal (left scale)

Differential with Germany, 3-month rate (right scale)

B. Exchange rate
January 1988 = 100

Trade-weighted

Against the ECU

Against the deutschemark

C. Index of monetary conditions[1]
January 1988 = 0

1. Index constructed by the Bank of Finland using a weighted average of changes in the 3-month money market rate (0.70) and in the effective exchange rate (0.30).
*Source:* Bank of Finland; OECD, *Main Economic Indicators.*

in official reserves which occurred in the first half of 1994 largely reflected public sector foreign-currency borrowing and associated capital imports (Diagram 14, Panel B).

Overall, therefore, it appears that monetary policy has eased considerably since the floating of the exchange rate. A useful gauge of the extent of such an easing is provided by movements in the Bank of Finland's Index of Monetary Conditions (Diagram 13, Panel C) – a weighted average of changes in the three-month money market rate[7] and in the trade-weighted exchange rate (relative to a

Diagram 14. **CENTRAL BANK INTERVENTIONS AND FOREIGN EXCHANGE RESERVES**
Billion markkaa

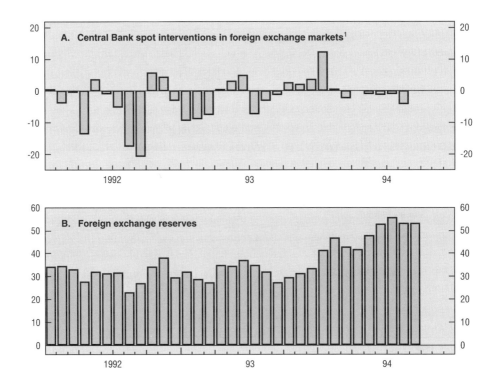

1. Negative values indicates sales of foreign currencies.
*Source: Bank of Finland Bulletin.*

base year).[8] This index suggests a substantial monetary relaxation in the aftermath of the floating, followed by relatively stable monetary conditions since mid-1993.[9]

Following the floating of the markka, long-term interest rates also fell from over 14 per cent in September 1992 to a 6½ per cent low in February 1994 (Diagram 15, Panel A). As a result, the long-term interest differential *vis-à-vis* Germany was gradually reduced, bottoming at 100 basis points in February 1994 (Diagram 15, Panel B). However, the OECD-wide jump in long-term interest rates that started in the spring of 1994 was particularly pronounced in Finland: by the beginning of November 1994 the five-year bond yield had risen to around 10 per cent, more than 200 basis points above equivalent German rates. While this is partly a reflection of turbulence in the Swedish bond market, worries about Finnish government finances have probably also contributed.[10] The yield-curve thus steepened considerably and, with inflation still subdued, the real long-term rate is now far above its historical average (Diagram 15, Panels A and C).

## Bank profitability and credit growth

With the emerging recovery, the crisis of the Finnish banking system – which resulted from the bursting of the 1980s strong credit boom – appears to be dissipating. For the first time since the beginning of the crisis in 1991, overall bank credit losses (on loans and guarantees) declined in 1993, amounting to Mk 19 billion – *i.e.* 2.5 per cent of the total assets of the banking sector (Diagram 16). This reflects a steep fall in corporate bankruptcies from their peak in late 1992, in line with the substantial easing of monetary conditions. In addition, the stock of banks' non-performing loans – which remains concentrated in the real estate and retail trade sectors – stabilised in 1993, to 4.5 per cent of total bank assets.[11]

These developments have led to a slight increase in bank earnings, thus contributing to some improvement in bank profitability during 1993. According to most recent available information, such an improvement seems to have continued, although at a more modest pace, into 1994. Indeed, even though net interest and other operating earnings have been declining, bank profitability has remained on an upward trend owing to a further reduction in credit losses.[12]

Domestic credit expansion continued to be sluggish, as evidenced by a decline in bank lending by almost 10 per cent both in 1993 and in the first half

Diagram 15. **LONG-TERM INTEREST RATE DEVELOPMENTS**

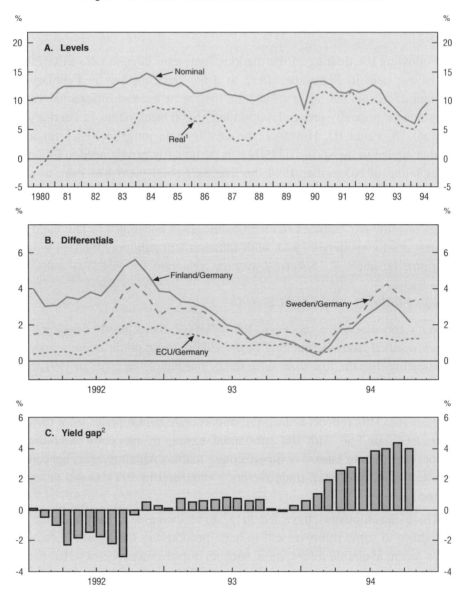

1. 5-year bond yield less the expected rate of inflation, the latter being measured by the percentage change on the GDP deflator over the 4 quarters following each observation.
2. 5-year Government bond minus 3-month money market rate.
*Source:* OECD, *National Accounts, Main Economic Indicators*, Secretariat estimates.

Diagram 16. **PROFITABILITY OF DEPOSIT BANKS**
Billion markkaa

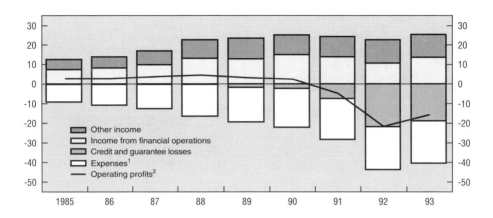

1.   Including depreciation.
2.   Gross of extraordinary items and taxes.
*Source:*   Bank of Finland.

of 1994, as compared with the same period a year earlier (Diagram 17, Panel A). Weak domestic demand and private sector financial consolidation appear to be the main factors behind this development. Indeed, most recent business surveys show a marked decline in the number of firms reporting borrowing difficulties.[13] Bank lending attitudes seem to have become more cautious though. In particular, collateral requirements for loans to households and smaller enterprises have been reinforced. However, there is no clear evidence of banks increasing profit margins in order to improve balance sheets: while the spread between average lending rates on new loans and money market rates widened from late 1992 to early 1994,[14] the difference between lending rates and deposit rates has remained remarkably stable since 1988.

## *Behaviour of money aggregates*

Growth of money aggregates has been accelerating in 1993 and 1994 (Table 11), in line with the revival of economic growth. The increase in M1

37

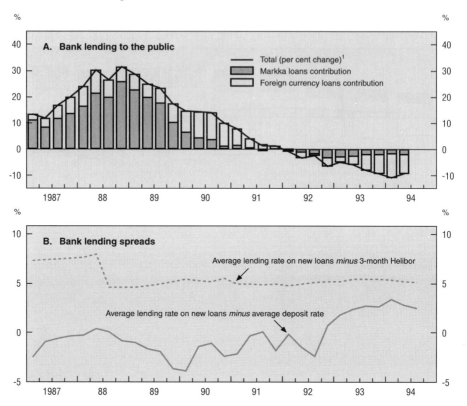

Diagram 17.  **INDICATORS OF CREDIT BEHAVIOUR**

1.   Over corresponding quarter of previous year.
*Source:   Bank of Finland Bulletin.*

during 1994 has been particularly rapid. While pointing to stronger economic activity, this is also due to a fall in interest rates on time deposits, which significantly reduced the opportunity cost of holding narrow money. In addition, there has been a shift into liquidity from bond holdings due to increased uncertainty in the bond market. Although the broad aggregates M2 (M1 plus time deposits) and M3 (M2 + certificates of deposit) have been boosted by significant increases in net foreign assets, this has to a large extent been offset by a fall in the stock of domestic credit.

Table 11. **Money growth**

Percentage changes

|  | 1990 | 1991 | 1992 | 1993 | 1994[1] |
|---|---|---|---|---|---|
| M1 | 13.9 | −7.7 | 3.2 | 5.1 | 8.9 |
| M2 | 5.9 | 3.3 | −0.4 | 2.0 | 3.8 |
| M3 | 6.8 | 6.8 | −0.1 | 3.8 | 4.6 |
| Contributions to M2 growth | | | | | |
| Foreign assets, net | −9.5 | −1.4 | 6.7 | 15.4 | 10.0 |
| Domestic credit | 17.9 | 11.1 | −8.8 | −12.6 | −10.4 |
| Other items, net | −2.5 | −6.4 | 1.7 | −0.8 | 4.2 |

1. For aggregates M1 and M3, growth over the period December 1993 to September 1994 at annualised growth rates. For contributions to the growth of M2, and M2 itself, growth from December 1993 to August 1994, also at annualised rates.
*Source:* Bank of Finland.

# Progress in structural reform

Following the substantial reforms introduced in the late 1980s and early 1990s in the fields of taxation, competition policy, the public sector and social security, a number of additional structural initiatives have been taken recently by the Finnish authorities. They include measures focusing on the implications of possible membership to the European Union (EU), as well as specific action concerning industrial policies, the banking sector and the functioning of the labour market. These measures are reviewed below. Structural policy changes designed to correct deficiencies in the control of public spending, notably with respect to the welfare state, are discussed in more detail in the next chapter.

## *Measures related to EU membership*

The regulatory reforms carried out in the context of the 1992 European Economic Area Agreement, which have been discussed in previous surveys, have brought Finnish legislation into broad conformity with the requirements of EU membership. The major remaining areas of adjustment relate to agricultural subsidies and indirect taxation where some measures have already been adopted. In addition, accession to the EU will broaden the scope of regional policies.

Immediately after the European Parliament approved, in May 1994, the treaties that Finland and other applicant countries negotiated with the EU members, the Finnish government presented an agricultural package with effect from

1 January 1995, ensuring compatibility with the common *agricultural policies* (CAP) of the EU.[15] The thrust of the package is to reduce production based subsidies to EU levels and to remove all import barriers towards other EU countries. This will imply substantial adjustments since:

  *i)* the level of government assistance in Finnish agriculture is relatively high. Gauged by the Producer Subsidy Equivalent (PSE),[16] it was, in 1993, 40 per cent above the average of EU countries, a level only matched by Norway among the OECD countries (Table 12);

  *ii)* to a larger degree than other Nordic applicants to EU (Norway in particular), Finland relied on extensive import barriers as a measure to support farmers' incomes.

In adjusting to the CAP, therefore, agricultural producer prices in Finland will have to drop significantly. This has prompted the government to propose, as part of the package, direct income support measures amounting to Mk 6½ billion in the first year to compensate for the expected fall in agricultural incomes (Table 13). As a result, direct aid to agriculture will rise from the present level of roughly Mk 35 000 per employed person in 1994 to Mk 85 000 in 1995 (excluding tax expenditures, see below).

Table 12.  **Agricultural support in Finland**

|  | 1991 | 1992 | 1993 |
| --- | --- | --- | --- |
| **Assistance to producers (PSE)** [1] | | | |
| Total Mk billion | 17.4 | 14.8 | 15.2 |
| Total US$ billion | 4.3 | 3.3 | 2.7 |
| Percentage of total gross output | 71.0 | 67.0 | 67.0 |
| Ratio of percentage PSE to: | | | |
| OECD countries | 1.69 | 1.63 | 1.59 |
| EU countries | 1.48 | 1.43 | 1.40 |
| Other EU applicants [2] | 1.09 | 1.06 | 1.08 |

1.  PSE: Producer Subsidy Equivalent. It measures the overall public support to a particular industry – including direct subsidies, import quotas, preferential tax treatment, etc. – as a percentage of value added.
2.  The other countries which applied for membership of EU with effect from 1995, namely Austria, Norway and Sweden.
*Source: Agricultural policies, markets and trade. Monitoring and Outlook,* OECD, 1994.

Table 13.  **Impact of EU-membership on the 1995 budget**

Changes from baseline, Mk billion

|  | Revenues | Expenditure | Increase in net "expenditure" |
|---|---|---|---|
| Agricultural policies | 1.3[1] | 6.5 | 5.2 |
| Structural funds[2] | 1.9[1] | 1.9 | 0.0 |
| Temporary revenues in transition period | 1.2 | – | –1.2 |
| Value added taxes, exercises and import duties | –0.3 | – | 0.3 |
| General transfers to EU[3] | – | 5.5 | 5.5 |
| Other | –0.1 | 0.5 | 0.6 |
| Total | 4.1 | 14.4 | 10.3 |

1.  Transfers from EU of 2.9 billions are partly offset by a loss in contributions from the agricultural sector of 1.6 billion markkaa.
2.  Expenditure and revenues associated with spending in Finland.
3.  Based on the total VAT-base and Gross National Income in Finland.
*Source:* 1995 Budget proposal.

Preliminary studies suggest that EU-membership would have a significant effect on the Finnish agricultural sector: with an estimated fall in prices of on average 40 per cent in 1995, incentives to produce will be markedly reduced as the income support measures are largely unrelated to output levels. As a result, agricultural income is officially expected to decline by about 20 per cent over the medium term. To facilitate the process of structural adjustment in agriculture – *e.g.* merging smaller farms into larger units and diversifying production activities – the 1995 Budget proposes some measures aiming at raising profitability, including a lowering of wealth taxes on farm assets and a continuation of interest rate subsidies on agricultural loans.

Measures have also been adopted to adjust the system of *indirect taxes* towards an EU-type value added tax (VAT). With effect of 1 June 1994 services have been included in the VAT base, implying that the reform of indirect taxation is now practically completed. Nonetheless, some further adjustments are envisaged in the 1995 Budget proposal, with virtually no net impact on indirect tax proceeds. The main change, with effect on 1 January 1995, is the abolition of the "primary product allowance", an indirect tax break aiming to lower food prices for Finnish consumers. This allowance will be replaced by the introduction of a reduced VAT rate of 17 per cent for food products (to be lowered to 12 percent in 1998; the standard VAT rate is 22 per cent) in 1995. Finland will maintain high levels of excise taxes on tobacco and alcoholic beverages, currently exceeding by far those prevailing in the Community. In this context, the Finnish government agreed with the EU on a provision restricting imports of such products, by travellers entering Finland, to quantities corresponding to levels "for personal use". However, in the future some downward pressure on the rates of these excise taxes could develop from increased cross-border consumer trading, depending upon developments in this area in neighbouring countries.

With EU membership, Finland will obtain access to EU funds for *structural adjustment*, representing a support of about Mk 2 billion per year in 1995 and beyond (Table 13). However, this support will be conditional upon the nature of the industrial and regional programmes to be financed that way and on their consistency with EU criteria. This may call for some restructuring of existing domestic programmes of this kind towards more transparent objectives. The EU structural aid package will include support for "arctic regions"[17] where presently about 16 per cent of the population lives. The assistance to these regions, which will be targeted toward job creation – using for example investment subsidies – and the development of infrastructure, is expected to amount to Mk 600 million per annum. Although activity in these regions is mainly related to agriculture, the support will not be restricted to this sector.

## Industrial policy

A general reorientation of Finnish industrial policy towards more market based principles is currently under way. It includes a privatisation and deregulation programme as well as a review of industrial subsidies.

### Privatisation and deregulation

State involvement in the business sector through direct ownership of enterprises is relatively large in Finland. In 1992, around 16 per cent of workers in the manufacturing and energy sector were employed by state-owned companies, while the equivalent figure in transportation and communication was 41 per cent (Table 14). Budgetary constraints, and the recognition that public ownership may hamper the necessary restructuring of companies in a context of enhanced international competition, led the government to launch a large privatisation programme in 1991. The implementation of this programme was adversely affected by the weakness of the Finnish stock market until early 1993. Subsequently,

Table 14.   **Employment share of state-owned enterprises in the business sector**

1992

| | Number of people employed | Percentage share of the industry's employment | Percentage share of total employment |
|---|---|---|---|
| Agriculture and forestry | 3 881 | 2.0 | 0.2 |
| Manufacturing and energy | 75 276 | 16.0 | 3.5 |
| Transport and communication | 67 566 | 41.0 | 3.1 |
| Trade | 4 124 | 1.0 | 0.2 |
| Restaurants and hotels | 555 | 1.0 | 0.0 |
| Financing | 6 545 | 3.0 | 0.3 |
| Other services | 2 217 | 0.0 | 0.1 |
| Total | 160 164 | 7.4 | 7.4 |

*Source:* Ministry of Finance and *National Accounts.*

however, the government intensified its action in this field, and in 1993 obtained Parliamentary authorisation for extending the scope of its original plan for privatisation.

As illustrated in Diagram 18, eleven state companies are now being listed for privatisation. All these firms are in the manufacturing and energy sector. The government is committed by Parliament to maintain either minority or majority stakes in the companies' share capital – with the exception of the forestry company Enso-Gutzeit, of which all state shares will be sold. Already, two companies – Valmet and Rautaruukki – have launched new share issues. It is the government's intention to proceed with the current programme of privatisation over the next two to four years, while at the same time preparing the ground for further action. It must be noted that, so far, there has been no initiative to privatise public companies in the transportation and communication sectors, which account for 3 per cent of the country's total employment (and where experience from other countries suggests that privatisation can provide substantial benefits). However, since 1 January 1994 the Posts and Telecommunications (PTT) have been transformed into a joint stock company with the government retaining full ownership; the same will be the case for the State Railways as of 1 July 1995.

In addition to privatisations, the government decided to initiate deregulation in the telecommunication market. As of 1 January 1994, private suppliers of long distance *domestic* telecom services have been allowed to operate. Moreover, with

Diagram 18. **SCOPE FOR PRIVATISATION**

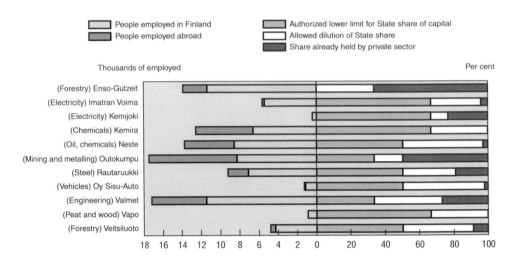

□ People employed in Finland
■ People employed abroad

▨ Authorized lower limit for State share of capital
□ Allowed dilution of State share
▨ Share already held by private sector

Thousands of employed                                                    Per cent

(Forestry) Enso-Gutzeit
(Electricity) Imatran Voima
(Electricity) Kemijoki
(Chemicals) Kemira
(Oil, chemicals) Neste
(Mining and metalling) Outokumpu
(Steel) Rautaruukki
(Vehicles) Oy Sisu-Auto
(Engineering) Valmet
(Peat and wood) Vapo
(Forestry) Veitsiluoto

18  16  14  12  10  8  6  4  2  0      20    40    60    80   100

*Source:* Ministry for Trade and Industry.

effect from 1 July 1994, two private suppliers of *international* telecommunication
services have been admitted to the market, which so far has been the exclusive
domain of the state-owned PTT. With these measures, the liberalisation of the
telecom industry in Finland appears to be progressing more than required by the
EEA and EU agreements.

*Industrial subsidies*

In contrast to agriculture (see above) government support to the private
business sector is rather limited compared to other EU countries, and has been
declining in recent years (Table 15). Indeed, direct subsidies and tax expenditure
to the manufacturing and service industries represented less than 1 per cent of
GDP in 1993. While the recent recession has triggered some additional direct
subsidies, this has been more than offset by a substantial decline in tax expenditures, largely resulting from the tax reform implemented in recent years.[18]

Table 15.  **Government industrial support**

Mk billion

|  | 1987 | 1988 | 1989 | 1990 | 1991 | 1992 | 1993 |
|---|---|---|---|---|---|---|---|
| Direct subsidies | 13.4 | 13.4 | 13.9 | 14.9 | 19.5 | 16.5 | 17.1 |
| *of which:* | | | | | | | |
| Agriculture | – | 9.5 | 10.0 | 10.7 | 12.1 | 11.3 | 10.6 |
| Manufacturing industries | – | – | 1.3 | 1.5 | 1.8 | 2.6 | 2.5 |
| Other | – | – | 2.6 | 2.7 | 5.6 | 2.6 | 4.0 |
| Tax expenditure, business sector | – | 48.7 | 43.9 | 36.9 | 30.3 | 29.5 | 27.0 |
| *of which:* | | | | | | | |
| Agriculture | – | 5.9 | 5.6 | 6.2 | 5.9 | 5.7 | 7.2 |
| Industry and services | – | 19.2 | 14.1 | 7.1 | 2.9 | 2.5 | 1.5 |
| Housing | – | 20.2 | 20.6 | 19.6 | 17.8 | 17.2 | 14.2 |
| Transport | – | 3.4 | 3.6 | 4.0 | 4.1 | 4.1 | 4.1 |
| *Memorandum items:* | | | | | | | |
| Subsidies as a per cent of GDP | 3.5 | 14.3 | 11.9 | 10.0 | 10.2 | 9.9 | 9.3 |
| *of which:* | | | | | | | |
| Direct subsidies | 3.5 | 3.1 | 2.9 | 2.8 | 4.0 | 3.5 | 3.6 |
| Tax expenditure, business sector | – | 11.2 | 9.0 | 7.2 | 6.2 | 6.3 | 5.7 |

*Source:* 1995 Budget proposal and Statistics Finland.

New initiatives announced in the 1995 Budget proposal focus on improving the quality of existing support programmes rather than cutting overall subsidy levels. The main objectives are: *i)* improving the evaluation and planning of support programmes through a more rigorous cost-benefit analysis; *ii)* specifying the duration of the programmes on a case by case basis, so as to avoid firms becoming dependent upon public funds; and *iii)* targeting subsidies on projects with a potentially high social return, for which private financing is seen as insufficiently available due to high financial risks. In this context, the Budget proposal envisages reducing support targeted on specific industries such as ship-building and publishing, while broadening the support programmes for research in small and medium-sized enterprises. Moreover, the government announced an in-depth review of the existing programmes in early 1995, which should be reflected in reform proposals in the 1996 Budget submission.

## Banking reform

With banks' profitability improving somewhat (see above), government's involvement in the banking sector has moved away from crisis management through direct support operations, to actions designed to prepare the grounds for a more efficient financial industry. In practice, these actions have sought to promote both a further rationalisation of the existing banking structure and strengthen bank supervision.[19]

Since early 1993, there have been no new direct injections of government money into banks' capital, except for the asset management company "Arsenal" (see below). Most of the government support operations have taken the form of guarantees aimed at strengthening banks' balance sheets. In 1993 and 1994, these guarantees totalled Mk 32 billion, bringing the amount of government support to the banks to Mk 75 billion (15 per cent of GDP) since the emergence of the banking crisis in 1991 (Table 16).[20]

With respect to rationalisation, the most important government action in 1993 was the restructuring of the Savings Bank of Finland, which was taken over by the state in 1992. The Savings Bank's non-performing assets (mainly loans) were grouped into a new government-owned asset-holding company, called "Arsenal", charged with winding down the loan portfolio through repayments or write-offs. In the context of this arrangement, the State offered a guarantee to Arsenal of Mk 28 billion to match the expected losses on the non-performing assets,[21] while – together with the Government Guarantee Fund[22] – injecting a total of Mk 5 billion of preferred share capital into that company; this was followed by a further capital injection of Mk 6 billion in 1994. The rest of the Savings Bank was sold, branch by branch, to the four major commercial banks – KOP, Union Bank of Finland, Postipankki (Postal Bank) and the Co-operative Banks – for a total sales price of Mk 5.6 billion.

As a result of this cession of the Savings Bank, the top four banks now account for 65 and 60 per cent of total bank deposits and loans, respectively, against 52 and 47 per cent 1992. With an expected further reduction of the lending activities of the Skopbank,[23] the banking sector is thus likely to become more concentrated in the future. This suggests that current policies towards rationalisation in the banking industry should also aim at limiting the scope for abuse of dominant positions in order to maintain competition through a closer monitoring of business practices in this sector. By enabling free cross border

## Table 16. **Banking support operations 1991-94**

### Mk million

| | Bank of Finland | Council of State | | | Government Guarantee Fund | | | Total |
|---|---|---|---|---|---|---|---|---|
| | | Preferred capital | Ordinary shares | Guarantees | Loans | Preferred capital [1] | Ordinary shares | |
| **1991** | | | | | | | | |
| SKOP Bank | 4 330 [2] | | | | | | | 4 330 |
| **1992** | | | | | | | | |
| SKOP Bank | 10 044 [2] | 580 | | | | 1 500 | 1 500 | 13 624 |
| Savings Bank of Finland | | 1 094 | | | | 8 500 | 2 900 | 12 494 |
| Co-operative Bank | | 1 108 | | | | | | 1 108 |
| Posti Pankki (Post Office Bank) | | 903 | | | | | | 903 |
| KOP | | 1 726 | | | | | | 1 726 |
| Union Bank of Finland | | 1 749 | | | | | | 1 749 |
| Other | | 582 | | | 500 | | | 1 082 |
| **1993** | | | | | | | | |
| SKOP Bank | −2 722 [2, 3] | 350 | | 300 | | 700 | | −1 372 |
| Savings Bank of Finland [4] | | −1 094 | 250 | | | −2 806 | 150 | −3 500 |
| STS – Bank | | | | | | 3 036 | | 3 036 |
| Arsenal Ltd. [5] | | | 3 442 | | | | 1 558 | 5 000 |
| KOP | | | | 1 800 | | | | 1 800 |
| Union Bank of Finland | | | | 1 000 | | | | 1 000 |
| Other | | | | 900 | −700 | | | 200 |
| **1994** | | | | | | | | |
| SKOP Bank | −1 820 | | | | 131 | | | −1 689 |
| Arsenal | | 6 000 | | 28 000 | | | | 34 000 |
| Savings Bank of Finland | | | | | | −454 | | −454 |
| **Total** | 9 832 | 12 998 | 3 692 | 32 000 | −69 | 10 476 | 6 108 | 75 037 |

1. Includes subordinated loans which may be included as tier two capital, thus boosting the BIS capital adequacy ratio.
2. The bank of Finland's support actions to Skop Bank have mainly been managed by three asset management companies owned by the Bank of Finland as the bank is legally prohibited from making direct capital injections.
3. Repayment of loans.
4. In 1993, the State and the GGF disposed of their shares in SBF, thus making net public injections into SBF negative for that year.
5. Arsenal Ltd. was established in 1993 to take over non-performing assets from SBF in conjunction with its privatisation, see text.

*Source:* Bank of Finland.

supply of banking services and removing restrictions on foreign ownership of banks, the EEA process, and subsequently EU membership, should help in this respect.

Rationalisation efforts in the banking sector have also been reflected in a significant reduction in the number of branches and of staff. Indeed, from 1989 to 1993, the number of bank branches, excluding post offices managed by Postipankki, has fallen from around 3 500 to 2 500, while, at the same time, the number of bank employees dropped by about a third (Diagram 19). However, a recent study suggests that overall banking ''capacity'' in Finland is still excessive.[24] In comparison with the other Nordic countries – which display a similar banking structure – the study finds that operating costs in Finnish banks are by far the highest, reflecting much higher number of staff, branches and automated teller machines. As a result, banking profitability in Finland appears to be the lowest among the Nordic countries. The Finnish Government could help correct these gaps by ensuring that those financial institutions largely dependent on State support go through the same rationalisation process as that currently being implemented by banks which do not benefit from any particular assistance.

As for supervision, with effect on 1 October 1993, a new body (the ''Financial Supervision Authority'') has been established, aimed at strengthening the monitoring of the banking sector. Two policy priorities have been set by this institution: *i)* changing bank lending practices; and *ii)* reforming the deposit guarantee scheme.[25] Recognising that banks have so far relied too much on solvency considerations when evaluating the creditworthiness of potential borrowers, the Authority envisages to encourage banks to put more emphasis on the expected cash-flow performance when making loan decisions, particularly in the case of large exposures. As regards deposit insurance, the aim is to reduce the scope of the present system where all deposits are fully covered, with no upper ceilings. The system is seen as imposing an open ended commitment upon the government, and potentially inviting bank managers to excessive risk-taking as they expect to be bailed out in case of insolvency. However, no specific legislation has yet been outlined by the Authority.

## *Labour market initiatives*

A few policy initiatives, aimed at enhancing labour market flexibility, have also been taken during the period under review. Important in this regard has been

Diagram 19. **RATIONALISATION IN THE BANKING SECTOR**

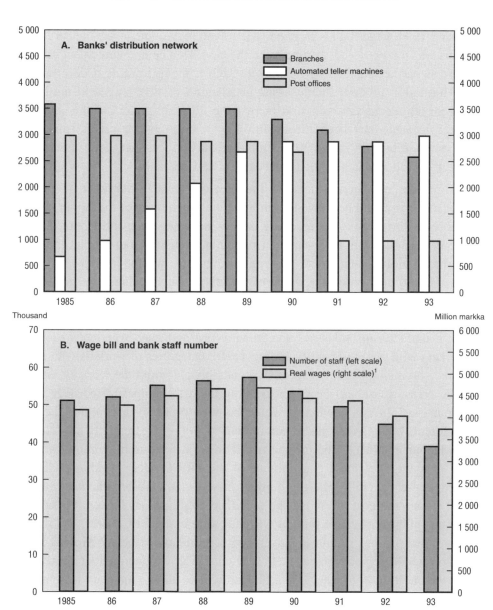

1. 1985 prices. The deflator used is the index of earnings in the private sector.
*Source:* Bank of Finland.

the government dissociating itself from private-sector wage negotiations, so as to encourage more decentralised and flexible wage determination. In effect, the 1993 and 1994 wage rounds essentially involved bargaining at the industry level, and this was not preceded, as used to be the case, by a central agreement between the social partners and the government. Such a move towards a decentralised wage formation process should assist in adapting relative wages to the highly divergent labour market conditions across the different sectors of the economy. Another measure has been the abolition of restrictions on private placement services, as stipulated in the 1994 Employment Services Act. This should contribute to a better matching of labour supply and demand.

However, as recommended in the previous OECD Survey of Finland,[26] further reforms would be needed to improve the functioning of the labour market, the more so since economic recovery is now gathering pace and labour demand in the private sector is increasing. In particular, active labour-market measures (including training, temporary job creation, etc.) – which, in 1994, involved about 100 000 persons or 4 per cent of the labour force – should be made more effective and better targeted towards emerging bottlenecks in the market. Such bottlenecks may arise even at relatively high levels of unemployment since, as noted, manufacturing industries are growing fast and may experience shortages of workers with particular skills. Moreover, for categories of workers with a high incidence of unemployment, especially young people with little work experience, specific measures should be taken to allow them to compete effectively in the labour market. In this context, it would be appropriate to discontinue the legal extension of wage agreements to non-unionised workers (essentially new entrants to the labour market).[27] The present restrictions on fixed-term employment contracts – among the most constraining in the OECD area[28] – should also be relaxed. More generally, the tax burden on wages should be alleviated, as this would reduce the cost of labour and stimulate employment. Indeed, Finland has one of the highest marginal rates of wage taxation in the OECD area, and there is evidence that this has significant adverse effects on employment.[29] Moving in this direction would require, however, further cuts in government expenditure. This raises the question as to what extent Finland will be able to maintain its relatively generous universal welfare system, an issue addressed in the next Part of the Survey.

# III.   The future of the welfare system

By extending the scope of its welfare system during the 1980s, Finland has gone further than most OECD countries in its efforts to achieve far-reaching social objectives through government action. While the budgetary consequences of this orientation went largely unnoticed as long as the economy grew rapidly, they surfaced in the early 1990s as the profound recession caused a dramatic surge in unemployment. As a result, the number of claimants of social transfers soared and public expenditure rose substantially. At present, general government welfare expenditure – including unemployment benefits, pensions, health care, education, social services and cash benefits – represents more than one-third of GDP and around three-quarters of total government non-interest spending (Diagram 20). This is high by OECD standards (Table 17), although comparable to levels seen in other Nordic countries.

Given the mounting state debt, these developments have highlighted the necessity for changes in current social entitlement programmes, with a view to strengthening the budget consolidation process and preserving competitiveness to prepare the ground for full participation in European integration. The need for sustained savings in welfare expenditure is generally acknowledged by the Finnish authorities, who, as part of their medium-term budgetary framework, have pledged to reduce total real government spending to its 1991 level by 1995. Nonetheless, official long-term projections suggest that – barring further reform in this area and in view of demographic developments – government finances will be over-burdened by the welfare system in the foreseeable future. Moreover, some of the institutional features of the system, as well as the high tax burden associated with it, have created rigidities and distortions which prove detrimental to economic growth. Hence the need for reforming the system on a broader basis.

After a brief review of the main characteristics and overall performance of the welfare system in Finland, this chapter first examines the cost of the system and its sustainability in the future. It then discusses the problems related to the

Diagram 20. **TRENDS IN WELFARE EXPENDITURE**
Per cent of GDP

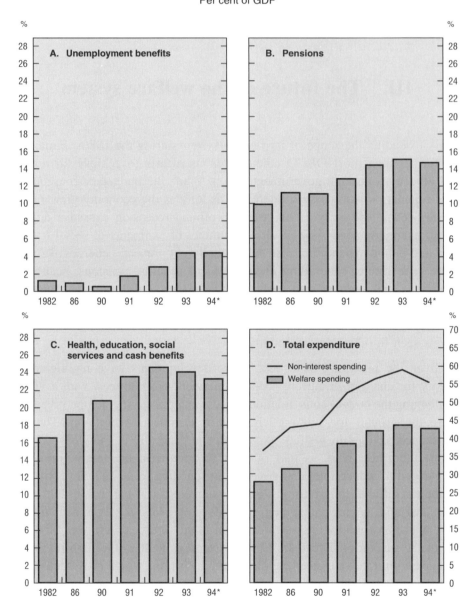

52

Table 17. **Structure of government outlays**
Per cent of trend GDP

| | Finland | | | Other Nordic[1] | | | OECD-Europe[2] | | | OECD[3] | | |
|---|---|---|---|---|---|---|---|---|---|---|---|---|
| | 1979 | 1991 | Percentage change | 1979 | 1990[4] | Percentage change | 1979 | 1990[4] | Percentage change | 1979 | 1990[4] | Percentage change |
| **I. Public goods** | **4.8** | **5.6** | **0.8** | **9.7** | **9.4** | **-0.4** | **8.8** | **8.5** | **-0.3** | **8.4** | **8.3** | **-0.1** |
| *of which:* | | | | | | | | | | | | |
| Defense | 1.3 | 1.5 | 0.2 | 2.9 | 2.7 | -0.2 | 2.8 | 2.5 | -0.2 | 2.8 | 2.7 | -0.1 |
| General public services | 2.9 | 3.3 | 0.3 | 4.3 | 4.7 | 0.4 | 4.7 | 4.8 | 0.1 | 4.3 | 4.4 | 0.1 |
| **II. Welfare** | **25.8** | **35.3** | **10.5** | **34.3** | **36.6** | **2.3** | **31.9** | **32.9** | **1.0** | **28.3** | **29.0** | **0.8** |
| *of which:* | | | | | | | | | | | | |
| Education | 4.9 | 5.5 | 0.6 | 6.8 | 6.5 | -0.3 | 6.1 | 5.5 | -0.5 | 5.8 | 5.3 | -0.6 |
| Health | 3.8 | 4.9 | 1.1 | 6.8 | 6.4 | -0.3 | 5.8 | 5.9 | 0.1 | 5.2 | 5.3 | 0.1 |
| Pensions | 8.8 | 12.4 | 3.6 | 9.2 | 10.2 | 1.0 | 9.8 | 10.1 | 0.3 | 8.5 | 8.9 | 0.3 |
| Sickness benefits | 0.5 | 1.3 | 0.8 | 2.3 | 2.9 | 0.6 | 1.5 | 1.7 | 0.2 | 1.1 | 1.3 | 0.2 |
| Family allowances | 0.8 | 1.5 | 0.7 | 1.6 | 1.9 | 0.3 | 1.7 | 1.6 | -0.1 | 1.5 | 1.4 | -0.1 |
| Unemployment benefits | 0.6 | 1.6 | 1.0 | 1.1 | 1.6 | 0.5 | 1.0 | 1.5 | 0.5 | 0.9 | 1.2 | 0.4 |
| **III. Economic services** | **8.6** | **8.7** | **0** | **8.0** | **7.0** | **-0.9** | **7.3** | **6.6** | **-0.7** | **6.9** | **6.1** | **-0.8** |
| **I-III. Non-interest expenditure** | **39.2** | **49.3** | **10.1** | **51.9** | **52.9** | **1.1** | **48.1** | **47.8** | **-0.3** | **43.4** | **43.4** | **-0.1** |
| **IV. Interest on public debt** | **0.9** | **1.7** | **0.8** | **3.7** | **5.3** | **1.6** | **3.2** | **4.4** | **1.2** | **3.1** | **4.4** | **1.4** |
| **I-IV. Total expenditure** | **40.1** | **51.0** | **10.9** | **55.6** | **58.2** | **2.7** | **51.3** | **52.2** | **0.9** | **46.5** | **47.8** | **1.3** |
| **V. Net lending** | **0.4** | **-1.5** | **-1.9** | **-0.1** | **1.1** | **1.2** | **-1.5** | **-1.3** | **0.2** | **-1.6** | **-1.0** | **0.6** |

*Note:* Aggregates for groupings are unweighted averages.
1. Denmark, Norway, Sweden.
2. Nordic countries plus Austria, Netherlands, Germany and U.K.
3. OECD-Europe plus United States, Japan, Australia.
4. Or most recent data.
*Source:* OECD.

institutional deficiencies and lack of proper incentive structures of individual welfare programmes. The scope for reform is finally addressed by identifying the main areas where further action is needed on top of recent initiatives already taken.

## Key features of the system

As in other Nordic countries, the welfare system in Finland includes a wide range of programmes, each of which targets specific needs of a particular segment of the population. In practice, however, a distinction can be made between social benefits for income replacement related to the labour market (unemployment and retirement benefits) on the one hand, and the provision or subsidisation of "merit goods" (health care, education and social services) on the other. Within these two broad categories various programmes co-exist, which are described below.

### *Income replacement programmes*

#### *Unemployment compensation*[30]

A central feature of the Finnish unemployment compensation scheme is its universality. All residents seeking a job are in principle entitled to either earnings-related unemployment insurance benefits, to the flat-rate basic Unemployment Allowance or, if other entitlements are exhausted or not applicable, to the means tested "Labour Market Support" (Table 18).

The *Unemployment Insurance* (UI) scheme provides unemployment benefits to job seekers who have paid contributions into one of the 71 occupational Unemployment Funds, almost exclusively managed by the trade unions, which represent 1.8 million members in total. The *Unemployment Allowance* (UA) scheme, which is managed by the local offices of the national Social Insurance Institution, provides benefits to job seekers who do not qualify for Unemployment Insurance (people who are not insured with one of the Unemployment Funds), including the previously self-employed. Both schemes require that claimants are available and applying for full-time employment, are registered as unemployed, and held a job for at least six months in the preceding two years. Payment of benefit also implies that a place in a job creation or training programme could not be offered by the employment office.

Table 18. **Income replacement for job seekers**

1994

| | Unemployment Allowance (UA) | Unemployment Insurance benefits (UI) | Labour Market Support[1] (LMS) |
|---|---|---|---|
| **Eligibility** | Record of employment for at least 6 months during the previous 2 years[2] | Record of employment for at least 6 months during the previous 2 years<br><br>Members of unemployment funds | No previous employment required<br><br>Persons falling outside the UA and the UI |
| **Benefits** | Basic daily amount (= Mk 116) | Basic daily amount + 42 per cent of difference between previous daily wage and basic amount up to an insured monthly wage of Mk 10 440, and 20 per cent of the exceeding amount | Basic daily amount (= Mk 116) |
| **Means testing** | No[3] | No | Yes[4] |
| **Duration** | 500 days[5,6] | 500 days[6] | Unlimited (up to age 65) |
| **Waiting period** | 5 days | 5 days | 3 months (except for those seeking a job immediately after graduation from university, etc.) |
| **Number of beneficiaries (1992)** | 192 000 (5.3% of w.a.p.)[7] | 268 000 (7.3% of w.a.p.)[7] | |

1. Took effect in 1994.
2. Employment requirement became effective in 1994.
3. Until 1994 means-testing was applicable.
4. Means-testing is not applied to persons enrolled in active labour market programmes nor, in the first 180 days, to persons who have exhausted their benefit entitlement under the UA or UI programmes.
5. Until 1994, benefits were paid for an unlimited duration.
6. The duration limit is not applicable for persons over the age of 55 to whom benefits are payable up to the age of 60.
7. W.a.p. stands for working age population.

*Source:* Ministry of Labour.

While the UI benefit consists of a basic amount supplemented by daily child and earnings-related allowances,[31] UA involves the basic amount (plus child supplement) exclusively. The maximum duration of the benefit under both

55

schemes is 500 days, without reductions in allowances over time, and no means tests are applied. However, unemployed persons aged over 55 are entitled to these benefits until the age of 60, after which they qualify for an unemployment pension (see below). Both the basic amount (including the child supplement) and the total benefit are subject to a ceiling, the level of which depends on the daily pay insured.[32] The UI replacement rate varies between 90 per cent, if previous monthly earnings amount to Mk 5 000 or less, and approximately 45 per cent, for previous monthly earnings of around Mk 20 000. A standard waiting period of five days applies to both the UI and UA schemes.

Since January 1994, first-time job seekers and persons who have exhausted benefit coverage under UA/UI are entitled to the *"Labour market support"* (LMS), managed (in common with UA) by the Social Insurance Institution. This new scheme supplements the Unemployment Allowance regime, which prior to January 1994 granted benefits on a means-tested basis with indefinite duration. The UA system no longer includes means testing, while the benefit duration is now in line with that of UI benefits. The LMS is a social assistance programme of last resort, with only the basic amount and child supplement granted, subject to means testing, and with indefinite duration. The means test evaluates the claimant's income as well as a portion of spouse income.[33] People who participate in training and rehabilitation programmes also receive this allowance, but are not subject to a means test. The standard waiting period in this scheme is three months; however, no waiting period is applied to those entitled to LMS after the expiration of UA/UI benefits, the allowance being payable without means test for the first 180 days.

The unemployment compensation system has increased in generosity over the past two decades (see Box 2). The introduction of the UA programme in 1971 raised benefit rates and made coverage universal and duration indefinite. UI and UA benefits were increased but made taxable in 1985. In 1989 the regulation requiring UI benefits to be cut by 12.5 per cent after 200 days was rescinded. Parallel to the enhancement of passive programmes, active programmes were expanded: with the 1987 Employment Act, the government became legally committed to providing either a job or training to youth and long-term unemployed, but this commitment was removed in 1992.

Box 2. **Income replacement programmes in Finland: a chronology of reforms**

1971        **Unemployment pension** introduced, minimum age set to 60 years.

1972        Previous systems of social welfare and non-insurance based unemployment compensation merged into a new system, providing an **Unemployment Allowance** (UA) not conditional on the employment record and given indefinitely, subject to means-testing.

1977        Duration of benefits in **Unemployment Insurance** (UI) increased from 150 to 200 days within one calendar year (this corresponds to coverage for nine to ten months per calendar year). The total maximum duration remained unchanged at 450 days.

1978        Age limit of unemployment pension reduced to 58 years.

1980        Age limit of unemployment pension reduced to 55 years.

1982        The levels of sickness and maternity allowances as well as work-related Accident Insurance benefits were raised and made taxable.

1983-1985   Major overhaul of the pension system:
            – Means testing of basic old-age retirement pensions under the National Pension Scheme (NPS) is removed, and benefit levels are made dependent upon benefits received from the Employment Pension Schemes (see Table 19).
            – Pension levels are raised and made taxable. A special tax threshold is introduced corresponding to the level of the basic NPS pension.
            – Age limit of unemployment pension raised to 60 years (fully effective from 1991 due to transition period).

1985        Complete overhaul of unemployment income support system, implying that:
            – Benefits of both UI and UA are made taxable.
            – The previous flat rate UI system becomes earnings related, and benefits are significantly raised, both on a gross and after tax basis (Diagram 25).
            – UI duration limit of 200 days per calendar year is removed, though with a 20 per cent reduction in benefit level after 100 days.
            – UI eligibility criteria are weakened as the reference period for the requirement of six months of employment is extended to include the last two years (previously only last six months included).

1986        Capital income is exempted when calculating pensioners' entitlement to means-tested supplementary benefits.
            Introduction of an **"early" disability pension** for person of 55 years or more and an old-age early retirement scheme for people aged 60 (58 for civil servants).

1987        Duration of UI extended to 500 days, full benefit period increased to 200 days, and the reduction of benefit level is now only 12.5 per cent.
            Introduction of part-time pension to persons aged 60 years.

*(continued on next page)*

(continued)

| | |
|---|---|
| 1989 | Full benefits paid during the *whole* duration of UI. |
| 1993 | Retirement age for public sector employees raised to 65 years (as for private sector employees). |
| | The target level for public pension lowered from 66 to 60 per cent of highest pre-retirement earnings (as for private sector employees). The change will be implemented gradually. |
| | Employers' (occupational) and UI pension contributions introduced. |
| | Pensioners' contributions introduced for the NPS. |
| | Employees' contributions introduced for UI. |
| 1994 | Eligibility for UA now requires six-month work experience within the last two years and duration is limited to 500 days, and means-testing is removed (basically same system as UI, though with a flat rate benefit). |
| | All first time job seekers, and unemployed who have exhausted their benefits coverage under the UI and UA, are now given a so called **"Labour Market Support"**. In this new scheme, the benefit level corresponds to the "old" UA system, Mk 116 per day which is means tested. |
| | All persons on active labour programmes will also be covered by this "new" transfer programme. |
| | Indexing of benefit levels are suspended. |

### *Retirement programmes*[34]

All Finnish citizens who have attained the legal retirement age of 65 automatically qualify for old-age pension benefits. In addition, various early retirement schemes exist which also are universal (Table 19). The distinction between unemployment and retirement benefits is therefore not always sharp, and in official Finnish reports specific early retirement benefits (such as the Unemployment Pension, see below) are usually labelled as unemployment-compensation rather than as retirement programmes.

Pension beneficiaries typically receive a flat-rate basic benefit under the *National Pension Scheme* (NPS), supplemented by an earnings-related occupational pension. The NPS, which is managed by the Social Insurance Institution, has universal coverage and aims at securing a basic (flat-rate) minimum income for the elderly, the disabled and some smaller specific groups such as survivors and front veterans. In addition, the scheme contains a number of early retirement

Table 19.  **Income replacement for retired people**
1994

| | Unemployment pension | Disability pension | Early disability pension | Old-age retirement pension |
|---|---|---|---|---|
| **Eligibility** | Age 60 years or older<br><br>Unemployment benefits received for 40 weeks during previous 60 weeks<br><br>No suitable job offer refused | Unfit for work compatible with age, skills, family ties, housing opportunities, etc.[1] | Age 58 years or older[1]<br><br>Working capacity reduced, but not necessarily unfit for work | Age 65 years (or older in case of deferred retirement)[2] |
| **Benefits** | | | | |
| A.  *National Pension Scheme* | See old-age retirement | See old-age retirement | See old-age retirement | Basic monthly allowance + a supplement which is inversely related to income from an occupational pension |
| B.  *Employment Pension Schemes* | See old-age retirement | See old-age retirement | See old-age retirement | 1½ per cent of average earnings over the last 4 years × number of contribution years -/- basic allowance[3] |
| **Beneficiaries (1992)** | 42 000 (1.2% of w.a.p.)[4] | 249 000 (7.3% of w.a.p.)[4] | 60 300 (1.8% of w.a.p.)[4] | 763 000 (15.3% of population) |

1.   Part-time early retirement is possible.
2.   An old age early retirement pension is possible for persons aged 60 or above; benefits are actuarialy reduced.
3.   Maximum benefit is 60 per cent of last earnings.
4.   W.a.p. stands for working age population.
*Source:* Central Pension Security Institute.

programmes, the most important ones being the so-called "Early Retirement Pension" and the "Unemployment Pension". The private and public sector *occupational pension schemes* provide earnings-related supplementary pensions to their members, topping up the pensions they draw from the NPS. Occupational schemes are administrated by various institutions under the close supervision of the Ministry of Social Affairs and Health, and participation is mandatory.

The eligibility requirements under the NPS and the occupational schemes are virtually the same, with *old-age pension* under both schemes granted when a worker has attained the legal pensionable age of 65. The amount of occupational old-age pension benefits depends on the length of the period of employment or self-employment and is vested over changes of employer. In the private sector, full pension rights require 40 years of employment, the rights accruing at a rate of 1.5 per cent per year of employment (before 1993 2 to 2.2 per cent in the public sector). The maximum pension, combining both the occupational pension and the basic amount of the national pension, is limited to 60 per cent of the highest pre-retirement earnings but deferred retirement involves higher benefits. However, part-time or full-time *early disability pensions* can be granted to a person aged 58, while old-age early retirement is possible from age 60 at an actuarially reduced pension benefit.[35]

Persons who have been unemployed for a considerable time are entitled to an *unemployment pension*, also combining a universal flat rate benefit granted by the National Pension Scheme and, if applicable, an earnings related supplement provided by the occupational pension schemes. The main eligibility requirements are that the person should be at least 60 years old (55 years until 1992, see Box), and has been receiving UI or UA during at least 200 days in the past 60 weeks, while no suitable job offer has been refused. The amount of the benefit is equal to the *disability pension*, which is granted to workers who suffer from reduced work capacity due to handicap, illness or injury, and whose incapacity to work is expected to last for at least one year. The labour market prospects of individual claimants, considering their age, skills and previous work experience, are also taken into account when deciding upon their enrolment in the disability pension.

## Funding methods

Two types of arrangements co-exist in financing income replacement pro-grammes (Table 20). First, under the Unemployment Security Act, the State finances the flat rate Unemployment Allowance and, since 1 January 1994, the Labour Market Support. The Unemployment Insurance and pension benefits are co-financed by the State, the employers and the employees, according to distribu-tive codes which are subject to negotiation rounds between the government and the social partners. The employees' share in the financing of occupational pen-sions has traditionally been very limited, and only in 1993 a contribution was

Table 20. **Financing arrangements of income replacement programmes**

1994

|  | Employees | Employers | State | Pensioners |
|---|---|---|---|---|
| **Unemployment allowance and labour market support** | – | – | 100% of total expenditure | – |
| **Unemployment insurance** [1] | 5.5% of total expenditure | 47% of total expenditure | 47.5% of total expenditure | – |
| **National Pension Schemes** | 1.6% of taxable income | 2.4-4.1% of private wage bill, 4% of public wage bill | – | Pensioners pay 1.6 of their taxable income, and in addition 1.0 per cent of their pension earnings |
| **Occupational Pension Schemes** | 3% of gross wage | ~ 16% of private wage bill ~ 18% of local government bill ~ 22% of state wage bill | – | – |

1. As the state's expenditure on unemployment benefits has risen dramatically with the recession, a special tax paid by all employees was introduced in 1993. It is calculated on the basis of gross wage income, accrues directly to the state and is not formally earmarked for transfers to the unemployment insurance system.
*Source:* Statistical Yearbook of the Social Insurance Institution, Finland.

introduced. The occupational pension schemes are partly funded, with around 75 per cent of the assets consisting of loans to the firms with which the funds are associated.[36] As, in the main, the occupational schemes were originally designed in 1962 under the Employees' Pensions Act (TEL), they are not yet mature, so that contributions to the schemes currently exceed benefits by 70 per cent.[37]

## Public services and income support

### Health care, education and social services

Local governments in Finland claim a relatively large part of total public resource use, due to the organisation of the key "merit goods" sectors (education, health and social services). Municipalities account for some 70 per cent of government employment and roughly 40 per cent of total government revenues and expenditures, in both cases well above the non-Nordic OECD average. The central government accounts for only 1 per cent of consumption and investment expenditure in health care, 6 per cent in social welfare services and 27 per cent (mainly on universities) in education (Table 21).

These patterns of public expenditure and employment reflect the dominance – typical in Nordic welfare systems – of local, public provision of health care, education and social services, primarily by local government employees. In *health care*, for example, Finnish law assigns to the roughly 450 municipalities[38] the responsibility to provide such services to all their citizens. However, the law allows considerable flexibility on how this is done. Municipalities may offer health services in their own institutions, they may form federations with other ones or they may purchase services from the private sector. In practice, the first two options dominate. The bulk of general medical treatment in Finland is carried

Table 21.  **Breakdown of government expenditure**

1993

| | General government Mk billion | Percentage share in total | | |
|---|---|---|---|---|
| | | Central government | Social security funds[1] | Local government |
| **Consumption and investment** | 125 | 34 | 3 | 63 |
| General administration and public order | 28 | 76 | – | 24 |
| Health care | 26 | 1 | – | 99 |
| Education and culture | 34 | 24 | – | 76 |
| Social welfare services | 22 | 6 | 15 | 79 |
| Infrastructure and business services | 15 | 80 | – | 20 |
| **Transfers** | 150 | n.a. | n.a. | n.a. |
| Households | 123 | 12 | 82 | 6 |
| Business | 16 | 100 | – | – |
| Other[2] | 11 | n.a. | n.a. | n.a. |
| **Gross interest payments** | 22 | n.a. | n.a. | n.a. |
| **Depreciation** | –8 | | | |
| **Total** | 289 | n.a. | n.a. | n.a. |
| *As a per cent of GDP* | 60.3 | n.a. | n.a. | n.a. |

1.  Includes occupational pension funds.
2.  Includes foreign development aid.
*Source: National Accounts* and OECD estimates.

out at municipal health centres, which are also in charge of maternity care, infant welfare, school health services, medical screening, vaccination and, occasionally, ambulance services and physiotherapy. Treatment in health care centres was until 1993 practically free of charge, but, if patients were hospitalised, charges did exist. Public hospitals are essentially managed by 21 federations of municipalities. Publicly-employed doctors can and do operate private practices, in which they are reimbursed on a fee-for-service basis by health insurers or by the patient. Private practitioners also have the right to refer patients to public hospitals. The private health sector is quite small.

Municipalities also run the primary and secondary *school system,* while central government is the main player as regards tertiary education (see above). Competition from private schools is virtually absent, although there are no regulatory barriers to entry. The absence of private schools would appear to be due to the fact that they are not eligible for public funds and that the public school system is of uniformly high quality. The *social services* cover a comprehensive system of day-care facilities provided mainly by municipalities, in which around half of the children in the age group from 0 to 6 years are enrolled – a feature which Finland shares with other Nordic countries. In addition, there are services for the mentally retarded, old people homes and ambulatory services for home help, such as nursing, cleaning, shopping etc. Around 20 per cent of the elderly receive such help – the highest number among the Nordic countries after Denmark. Charges paid by clients usually cover only a small fraction of the total cost of services. Private institutions also offer such services. They are supervised by local social welfare committees but not subsidised.

### Cash benefits

Cash benefits include rent subsidies (granting on average around Mk 10 000 per year to about 12 per cent of all families), child allowances (around Mk 8 500 per child under 17 per year) and advance payments of maintenance allowances agreed upon in connection with a divorce (around Mk 5 000 per year per household entitled to this type of benefit). In addition, as in all Nordic countries, Finland has an extensive system of benefits for people on leave for reasons of illness, pregnancy, childbirth or adoption. Depending on industry-specific collective bargaining agreements, workers receive one to two months of fully paid sick leave; universally, benefits for sick leave amount to 60

Table 22. **Local government revenue sources**

Mk billion

| | Before the grant reform (1992) | | | After the grant reform (1993) | | |
|---|---|---|---|---|---|---|
| | Total local government[1] | Municipalities | Federation of municipalities | Total local government[1] | Municipalities | Federation of municipalities |
| **State grants** | 43.4 | 31.0 | 12.4 | 41.7 | 40.8 | 0.9 |
| *of which:* | | | | | | |
| Non-earmarked | 1.5 | 1.5 | 0.0 | 38.5 | 38.5 | 0.0 |
| Earmarked for:[2] | | | | | | |
| Health | 12.7 | 3.5 | 9.2 | 0.7 | 0.0 | 0.7 |
| Social services | 11.8 | 11.0 | 0.9 | 0.0 | 0.0 | 0.0 |
| Education | 14.6 | 13.0 | 1.6 | 0.2 | 0.0 | 0.2 |
| Investment, etc. | 2.8 | 2.0 | 0.9 | 2.3 | 2.3 | 0.0 |
| **Local revenues** | 87.2 | 81.1 | 17.0 | 87.0 | 81.6 | 25.2 |
| *of which:* | | | | | | |
| Local income tax | 47.2 | 47.2 | – | 45.5 | 45.5 | – |
| Other local tax | 0.6 | 0.6 | – | 2.4 | 2.4 | – |
| Charges, fees, etc. | 22.3[3] | 17.4 | 15.7[3] | 23.3 | 18.7 | 24.4[3] |
| Investment income | 17.1 | 16.0 | 1.8 | 15.9 | 15.0 | 0.8 |
| **Total resources** | 130.6[3] | 112.2 | 29.4 | 128.7 | 122.4 | 26.1 |
| *As a per cent of GDP* | 27.4 | 23.5 | 6.2 | 26.7 | 25.6 | 5.4 |

1. Consolidated, that is net of transfers between municipalities and federation of municipalities.
2. Before the reform, earmarked grants covered 44 per cent of local health expenditure, 42 per cent of local social services and 49 per cent of local expenditure on education.
3. Includes payments from municipalities which in 1993 accounted for 80 per cent of the federations' income from charges, fees, etc.

*Source:* Ministry of Social Affairs and Health, Statistics Finland.

to 70 per cent of regular earnings, payable after a nine-day waiting period for a maximum period of one year. A maternity benefit is payable to women for approximately five weeks before childbirth and an additional parental benefit (granted to either the father or the mother) is paid for about 40 weeks after childbirth. Next to Sweden, this is the most generous scheme in the Nordic countries. A similar arrangement exists for adoption. The benefit level corresponds to that for sick leave, which is somewhat less generous than in other Nordic countries.

### Financing arrangements

Financing arrangements in the health, education and social services sectors are largely embedded in the overall financial relationships between the central and local authorities. Municipalities have a relatively large tax autonomy, although there are also significant transfers from central to local government in the form of state grants designed to co-finance the local welfare system (Table 22). The local income tax, which is levied on the same tax base as the state income tax, provided about one-third of total local receipts in 1991. While the rates are set freely, they do not vary much across municipalities; in 1993 they fluctuated within a range of 16 to 20 per cent of the local tax base. While another fifth of local government expenditure is financed by user charges, the remainder is covered by state grants, ensuring (legally required) balanced budgets. Before the grant system was reformed in 1993 (see below), it covered about 50 per cent of local government expenditure within the areas of health, education and social services. Aiming at high standards of public provisions across the country, irrespective of geographical differences in economic performance and wealth, grants were earmarked for specific purposes and their level was adjusted to cover the actual cost incurred. Since early 1993, grants are fixed in advance but no longer earmarked, providing the municipalities with a given budget which they can spend in ways they consider appropriate.

## Overall performance

As in other Nordic countries, the welfare system in Finland is generally considered to have been successful in achieving its social objectives. The system has managed to make the well-being of people largely independent of family

Table 23. **Selected indicators of welfare performance**[1]

| | Perinatal mortality | Infant mortality | Performance in reading at age 14[2] | Labour force participation of females | Poverty risk[3] | | Disposable income in relation to national mean | |
|---|---|---|---|---|---|---|---|---|
| | | | | | All households | Age group elderly | Age group 65 to 74 | Age group 75 or more |
| **Finland** | **0.59** | **0.52** | **109** | **70.7** | **3.7** | **1.5** | **0.90** | **0.82** |
| Other Nordic countries[4] | 0.65 | 0.61 | 102 | 76.3 | 5.0 | 2.4 | 0.99 | 0.79 |
| OECD Europe[4] | 0.81 | 0.71 | 100 | 53.3 | 6.0 | 7.0 | 0.92 | 0.79 |
| OECD[4] | 0.80 | 0.91 | 100 | 60.3 | 8.5 | 8.8 | 0.93 | 0.80 |

1. 1992 or latest data before 1992.
2. Index, OECD average is 100.
3. Percentage of households with income below one-half of the median household income.
4. Unweighted average.
*Source:* Government Institute for Economic Research (Finland) and OECD.

structures and prevailing market conditions. It has also been effective in limiting poverty and reducing income inequalities. For example, the generous programmes of income support and old-age pensions have contained the incidence of poverty and divided its risk more evenly across age groups (Table 23). Moreover, the comprehensive public health care system has contributed to a sound health situation in Finland, as evidenced by the very low rates of perinatal and infant mortality which are matched only by other Scandinavian countries and Japan. The system of low charge day-care facilities has helped open up career and other opportunities for women and has contributed to educational success by expanding learning opportunities for young children. Finally, as confirmed by a recent OECD study,[39] Finland has an education system of outstanding quality, maintaining uniformly high standards across the country and ranking first in international comparisons of reading performance of adolescents. However, these favourable outcomes must be assessed against the rising budgetary cost of the various welfare programmes, as discussed below.

## The rising cost of the system

### *Expenditure trends*

After a steady increase as a share of GDP during the 1980s, public welfare expenditure rose dramatically in the wake of the sharp recession of the early 1990s (Diagram 20). This trend masks diverging patterns in individual welfare programmes, however. The share of unemployment benefits in GDP fell from about 2 per cent in the early 1980s to around 1 per cent in 1990, and then quadrupled to around 4 per cent in 1994 due to the rising number of recipients of UA/UI benefits associated with the rapid increase in unemployment (Diagram 21). This increase would have been much stronger without the fall in unemployment outlays per recipient, which occurred as many low-paid workers (in particular young workers) became unemployed. Moreover, pensions for retired people, including the disabled and the unemployed permanently relieved from job-search requirements (unemployment pension), increased substantially throughout the 1980s and early 1990s, a trend which is expected to continue with population ageing (see below). By contrast, after a period of vigorous growth in the 1980s, expenditures on health care, education, social services and other transfers were held in check in the early 1990s, before being sharply reduced in

## Diagram 21. RECIPIENTS OF INCOME REPLACEMENT BENEFITS

Number of beneficiaries as a percentage of working age population

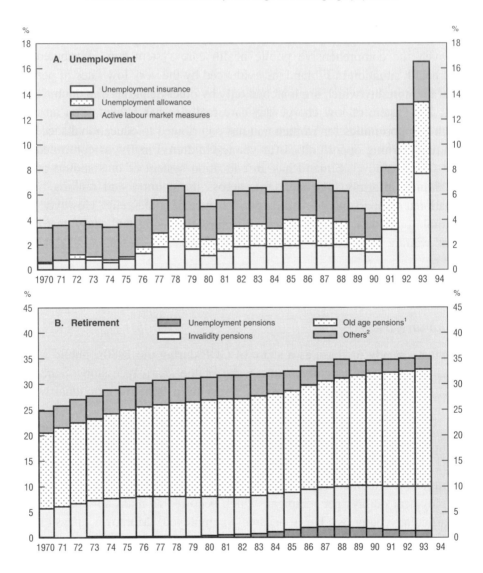

1. Including early retirement.
2. Survivors, orphans and miscellaneous.
*Source:* NOSOSO, Social Security in the Nordic Countries; *Statistical Yearbook of the Social Insurance Institution,*
1992 ; *Statistical Yearbook of Finland;* Submissions of the Ministry of Social Affairs and Health.

1993 and 1994, both in absolute terms and as a percentage of GDP, in an effort to keep public finances under control. This has resulted in a marked change in the composition of welfare expenditure, with unemployment and retirement transfers representing a much larger share of government outlays than before.

Compared with other OECD countries, the rise in welfare expenditure in the 1980s proved much stronger in Finland, where the ratio of welfare spending to trend GDP jumped from 26 per cent in 1979 to 35 per cent in 1991; during the same period, this ratio stayed practically constant in many other OECD economies (Table 17 above). Aside from the welfare system, "public goods" production, including defence, justice, development aid, etc., also absorbed increasing resources. As a result, the share of public employment through the 1980s rose from 18 to 22 per cent, a growth record in the OECD area matched only by Norway. By comparison, the share of public employment remained unchanged at around 17 to 18 per cent in OECD-Europe generally.

Prior to the depression of the early 1990s, the size of the welfare state in Finland, including spending on income transfers, health care and education, was broadly comparable to that in other Nordic countries.[40] On the other hand, total welfare expenditure significantly exceeded levels in other European economies (Table 17). Also, expenditure on "economic services" was somewhat higher in Finland than in the rest of Europe, largely reflecting agricultural subsidies (Part II). In the early 1990s, however, the share of welfare expenditure in (a falling) GDP increased rapidly, by an additional 10 percentage points (Diagram 20, Panel D), and is now among the highest in the OECD area.

## Long-run sustainability

Falling birth rates since the 1970s and increased longevity have reduced the growth of the Finnish population and changed its age composition. These demographic developments, which have been more acute than in most other OECD countries, will have widespread social and economic effects through their impact on labour markets, the structure of demand, saving and capital accumulation, as well as the cost of the welfare state. According to national projections, the old-age dependency ratio (population dependent upon income transfers as a percentage of the working age population) is bound to increase by substantial amounts (Diagram 22, Panel A). The adverse consequences of this evolution will already

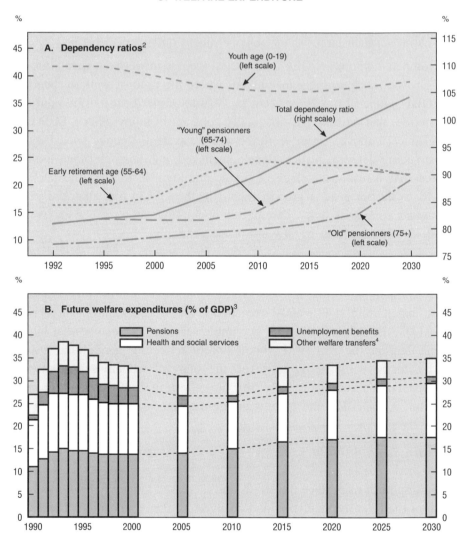

Diagram 22.  **LONG TERM PROJECTIONS OF WELFARE EXPENDITURE**[1]

1.  Child allowance, maternity leave, child home care allowance, child support, child care allowance.
2.  Population per age group as a percentage of the working age population (20-64).
3.  Excluding educational spending.
4.  Family allowances and benefits for illness and injury.
*Source: National Accounts, Statistical Yearbook of the Social Insurance Institution;* Government Research Institute (VATT); Ministry of Social Affairs and Health. "Sociaalimenotoimikunnan mientinto" (Social Expenditure Committee); OECD.

be evident in the next decade, when people from the post-war "baby boom" generation enter the age bracket relevant for early retirement (58 to 64). The situation will probably worsen after 2020, as the number of very old people (75 and above) is expected to increase while the youth dependency ratio, after a steep fall, returns to present levels.

A demographic shock of that size will inevitably have a large impact on welfare expenditure, particularly on social transfers, pensions and "merit goods". A recent report by the Committee on Social Expenditure of the Ministry of Social Affairs and Health[41] illustrates the potential cost pressures arising from such a shock. The projections shown in this report point to an initial fall in social spending (excluding education) from its present peak of 38 per cent to about 30 per cent of GDP in 2010 owing to a sustained economic recovery, followed by a rebound to 35 per cent in 2030 (Diagram 22, Panel B). This implies that the effects of an ageing population are strongly felt after 2010, with increased expenditure on pensions, health care and social services. These projections are based on a "high growth scenario", with rates of GDP growth of 3 to 4 per cent on average per year in the coming decade, generating a fall in unemployment to 5 per cent of the labour force by 2010. More pessimistic scenarios are presented as well in the report, but are seen as less realistic in view of the strength of the current recovery.

In order to assess the long-term implications of such developments in welfare spending on Finland's fiscal position, the Secretariat has carried out a simulation of the debt dynamics associated with the above projections of social expenditure.[42] The simulation assumes an unchanged tax share in GDP and unchanged real spending on education per person in the relevant age brackets.[43] While uncertainties are inevitably attached to such calculations, the results indicate that public debt, after temporarily stabilising at the unprecedentedly high level of about 95 per cent of GDP in the period 2000 to 2010, would become unsustainable in the following three decades (Diagram 23). The calculations therefore suggest that despite the budget consolidation efforts undertaken in the early 1990s (see Part II), Finland's future fiscal position will be heavily constrained by the growing costs of the welfare state.

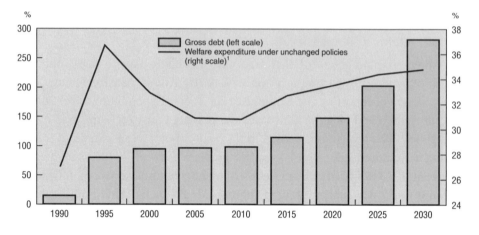

Diagram 23. **PUBLIC DEBT SIMULATIONS BASED ON PROJECTIONS OF WELFARE SPENDING**
Per cent of GDP

1. Includes education. Based on the Social Expenditure Committee projections (see also Diagram 22.B).
*Source:* OECD Secretariat.

## Problems with the management of the system

While the rising burden of the welfare system in Finland reflects, to a large extent, past government policies, it is also the result of a number of problems inherent in the functioning of the system. These relate to deficiencies in the existing budgetary planning procedures, to disincentives built into the income security scheme, and to the lack of cost efficiency considerations in the local provision of welfare services prior to the grant reform in 1993 (see below).

### Budget planning deficiencies

Faced with an increasing share of GDP going to public expenditure, the Finnish authorities introduced, in early 1991, a medium-term framework designed to improve the institutional setting of the budgetary process. As a result, the budget cycle now includes a medium-term planning round, allowing the government to impose expenditure ceilings for the three years following a budget year (Table 24). The spending ministries – including the Ministry of Social

Table 24. **Central government budget planning**

| Year[1] | Month | Action |
|---|---|---|
| **t – 2** | November-January | The Ministry of Finance (MoF) formally initiates a new planning round. |
| **t – 1** | January-February | Spending ministries draw up their medium-term plans and the MoF prepares its proposal for the expenditure ceilings for the years t, t + 1, t + 2 and t + 3. |
| | February-March | The government formally approves the medium term expenditure ceilings. |
| | April-May | The spending ministries formally approve their budget proposals. |
| | May-August | The preparation work takes place in the MoF and negotiations are held with spending ministries. |
| | August | The government formally approves the budget proposal. |
| | September | The budget proposal is given to Parliament. |
| | December | Parliament enacts the budget law. |
| **t** | January | Budget effective. |

1. Budget year = t.
*Source:* Ministry of Finance.

Affairs and Health which is largely responsible for the budgeting of welfare expenditure – make an input in this process, as they provide, for each round, updated medium-term spending projections, which are considered by the Ministry of Finance when fixing the expenditure ceilings in the budget proposal. These initial projections are essentially mechanical updates of previously agreed-upon medium-term targets in the current budget, allowing for the latest economic developments and recent changes in legislation. In line with this procedure, the initial projections submitted by the Ministry of Social Affairs and Health (whose budget covers the state contributions to the social security funds and the grants to local government), incorporates the impact of the expected unemployment figures on social expenditure. Current policies imply that the expenditure ceilings fixed on the basis of these initial projections must "add up" so as to rein back the aggregate level of real central government spending (including debt servicing costs) to its 1991 level by 1995.

While the adoption of this medium-term approach to budgetary policy making has helped to improve the planning process, it has not been reflected in reduced slippage in central government expenditure in the years 1991 to 1993 (Diagram 24, Panel A). There are three main reasons for this. *First,* as the

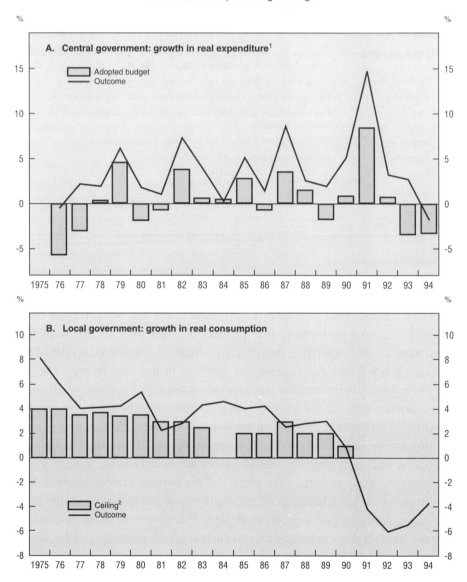

Diagram 24.  **EXPENDITURE PLANNING AND OUTCOMES**

Volumes, annual percentage changes

A.  **Central government: growth in real expenditure[1]**

Adopted budget
Outcome

B.  **Local government: growth in real consumption**

Ceiling[2]
Outcome

1.  Nominal expenditure has been deflated by the total domestic demand deflator.
2.  As agreed between the Ministry of Finance and the Association of Municipalities; see main text.
    In the period 1991 to 1994, no ceilings have been agreed.
*Source:*  Submission from the Ministry of Finance; OECD Secretariat.

recession turned out to be much deeper and longer than initially projected, social transfer expenditure rose much more than planned. *Second*, the scope of the medium-term expenditure ceilings still appears limited. Apart from some high-profile savings decisions made in 1991/92, the task of reconciling bids from ministries with the aim of cutting overall expenditure is left entirely to arbitration between the Ministry of Finance and individual ministries, without guidance from stated government priorities. This procedure encourages ministries to overbid and avoids making sensitive trade-offs between individual spending programmes. The end result has consistently tended to be an attribution of savings across ministries, with bids from ministries being cut by more or less the same proportion.[44] *Third*, the Parliament is not committed to approve the expenditure ceilings fixed by the government. This means that, during the budget discussion, the ceilings can be disregarded, particularly if the spending cuts proposed to meet the ceilings are not acceptable to the members of Parliament. This is made even more exacting by the fact that, constitutionally, enforcement of expenditure cuts affecting ''acquired social rights'' – which involve virtually all areas of welfare spending – require a two-thirds (and in some cases five-sixths) majority in the Parliament.

Another factor which has contributed to making expenditure growth higher than intended has been the functioning of the grant system for financing local welfare expenditure. As it operated before 1993, the system triggered semi-automatic participation from the State whenever the regional authority spent resources and had little built-in stimulus for serious cost-benefit trade-offs. While, until 1991, the Ministry of Finance and the Association of Municipalities attempted to curb local government expenditure by, *inter alia*, agreeing on targets for increases in total local government consumption, this proved to be largely ineffective, as these targets were consistently overshot by considerable amounts (Diagram 24, Panel B). The fact is that neither the central government nor the Association of Municipalities had any legal authority to impose sanctions if agreements were violated.[45] Moreover, as they enjoy tax autonomy, the municipalities are not entirely dependent upon state approval and grants for the financing of expenditure increases. Since 1991, however, this situation has changed due to the recession. While no new expenditure ceilings were agreed upon, the central government has cut the grants by significant amounts, forcing local government to reduce spending as the local tax base shrank. This trend has continued with the 1993 reform of the grant system, as discussed further below.

## Disincentive effects of income security

The steep rise in expenditure on unemployment benefits in recent years has revealed the costliness of the *unemployment compensation* system in an environment of substantial labour market slack. The generosity of the system has been an important factor in this regard. Indeed, both from the viewpoint of the duration of unemployment benefits and the associated replacement rates, the Finnish system appears to be one of the more generous among OECD countries (Diagram 25). When the means-tested housing allowances[46] and the child supplement contingent on unemployment benefits are included, replacement rates are often 80 to 100 per cent of take-home pay, so that people nearing the age at which they could apply for early retirement or an unemployment pension have very little incentive to continue working. Effective replacement rates sometimes even exceed 100 per cent. This may occur since, after a six-month spell of temporary employment (either in a regular or in a subsidised job), unemployed persons requalify for 500 more days of unemployment benefits at the same level as they were during the previous time of unemployment. This has resulted in perverse effects in sectors such as construction, where declining average wages have made that unemployment compensation is now often higher than net pay.

In addition, as currently designed, the income security system is susceptible to abuses on the part of beneficiaries. This arises because under present conditions of very high unemployment, the true willingness of unemployed people to seek a job – the key requirement for eligibility to unemployment compensation – is not effectively tested. Indeed, the very weak labour market has made it extremely difficult for authorities to distinguish between claimants seriously searching for a job and those preferring to stay unemployed. Likewise, the arrangements for unemployment compensation are exploited by some employers to finance temporary lay-offs, facilitated by the relatively short five-day waiting period. Indeed, numerous are the cases where employers regularly rehire dismissed workers after relatively short spells of unemployment.

The *pension system* also contains institutional features producing a tendency towards increasing costs – notably through attracting claimants for unemployment or invalidity pensions for whom these programmes were not designed. The main problem here concerns the method of accruals of occupational old-age pension rights. People receiving benefits under one of the above mentioned schemes accrue rights as if they were still employed. By contrast, old-age pen-

Diagram 25.  **REPLACEMENT RATIOS**

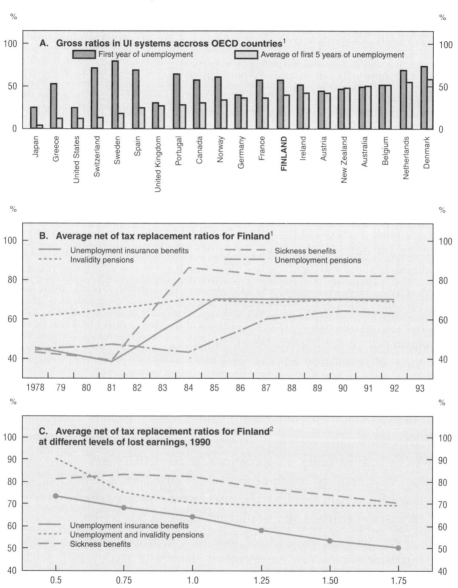

A.  **Gross ratios in UI systems accross OECD countries**[1]
First year of unemployment    Average of first 5 years of unemployment

B.  **Average net of tax replacement ratios for Finland**[1]
Unemployment insurance benefits    Sickness benefits
Invalidity pensions    Unemployment pensions

C.  **Average net of tax replacement ratios for Finland**[2] **at different levels of lost earnings, 1990**
Unemployment insurance benefits
Unemployment and invalidity pensions
Sickness benefits

1.  For a married worker with earnings equivalent to 85% of an Average Production Worker (APW).
2.  Income levels are defined as a multiple of the wage of a single APW.
*Source:*  Submissions from the Ministry of Social Affairs and Health; NOSOSO, Social Security in the Nordic Countries, 1993; *The OECD Jobs Study,* 1994.

sion accruals are discontinued for unemployed drawing an unemployment allowance, putting them at a disadvantage *vis-à-vis* beneficiaries of invalidity and unemployment pensions. Given the increasing share of long-term unemployment and the associated risk of losing pension rights, this feature clearly produces an incentive to apply for an unemployment or invalidity pension. In fact, after the minimum age for the unemployment pension was raised (see above), the number of new claimants fell, but only at the expense of rising numbers of people requesting invalidity benefits.

## *Lack of cost efficiency in local services*

The current level of *per capita health care* expenditure in Finland is roughly in line with that observed in the rest of the OECD area (Table 17) – notably when controlling for differences in real per capita GDP. However, *growth* in health expenditure in the 1980s and early 1990s has been more rapid in Finland than in any other OECD country apart from the United States and Canada (Diagram 26).[47] Finnish health expenditure has gradually shifted from in-patient to out-patient care, which, in theory, is favourable from a point of view of overall cost containment. Indeed, international comparisons suggest that countries which concentrate on ambulatory services tend to have lower per capita spending on health, as such services are typically less costly than in-patient care, *i.e.* a stay at a hospital.[48] The fact that Finland has, nonetheless, experienced relatively fast growth in expenditure may thus point to inefficiencies and/or a rising comparative service level.

While far from being a unique case in the OECD area with respect to difficulties in controlling health expenditure, Finland has a number of features which may help explain the relatively rapid increase in this category of spending. Three factors, in particular, are worth mentioning in this regard:

–   *First*, there is an apparent lack of competition between health-care providers, removing an important element of quality and, potentially, cost control. Patients are usually obliged to make use of the health service in the municipality of their residence, unless they are members of an occupational health service where they are employed. Municipalities thus favour their own institutions, and avoid payments for medical treatments elsewhere. Moreover, the system produces disincentives for a

Diagram 26.  **GROWTH IN HEALTH CARE EXPENDITURE BY COMPONENTS, 1980-1990**
Change in percentage points of trend GDP over period

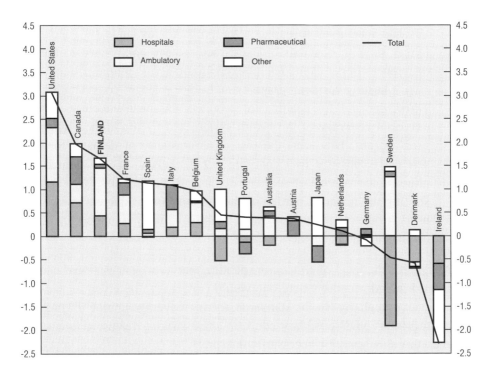

*Source:*  OECD Health Data.

more rational spread of resources across municipalities, for example from increased specialisation, thus contributing to excess capacity in a wide range of medical disciplines;

– *Second*, barring the impact of the new state grant system (see below), incentives to reduce costs in health institutions have been virtually absent. Until 1993, state grants to municipal health centres were based solely on historical costs.[49] Furthermore, since hospitals are mainly managed by federations of municipalities, the capacity to effect controls to improve efficiency have been weak. With almost 50 per cent of operational revenues drawing on state grants based upon costs incurred, there was also less incentive by municipalities to control costs. Since the remainder was financed by municipalities on the basis of "output" measures (*e.g.* number of hospital days and of out-patient visits), hospitals had incentives to expand "output", for example by encouraging longer stays in hospitals.[50] These factors have contributed to the wide differences in per capita health expenditure across municipalities – even after adjusting for demographics and other relevant considerations;[51]

– *Third*, demand for health care products has been encouraged by the universal coverage of the health system and by the limited reliance on user charges. However, the low price elasticity of demand for health services means that user charging is not likely to exercise much discipline on the volume of services demanded. Furthermore, by essentially shifting the financial burden of the system from taxpayers to individual users, extensive reliance on such charges is likely to undermine significantly the equity of the system.[52]

As regards the level of *education* spending per pupil, international comparisons place Finland roughly where one would expect it to be given its per capita income, even though, by Nordic standards, the high average number of pupils per teacher in primary and secondary education is a striking feature (Diagram 27). However, this should not be necessarily interpreted as evidence for an appropriate efficiency performance in education. It merely reflects the increase in the number of children in the relevant age group over the last decade, contrary to what happened in Sweden, Norway and Denmark in the same period. Finland has thus, at least on aggregate, not been confronted with the difficult task of cutting school staff to maintain stable pupil/teacher ratios.[53] Hence, while the cost per pupil may now be normal in comparison with other Nordic countries, it may rise in the future when the number of pupils in the relevant age group falls.

Operating as it does under the same type of funding as the public health sector, the basic school system is subject to similar drawbacks of increased pressure on spending. The system is indeed funded almost entirely with tax resources – small nominal tuition fees being levied exclusively in advanced education. Before the grant reform, the state automatically reimbursed the bulk of local spending on education, reducing incentives to economise on resource use. The effects of this set-up are evident from the wide variation in spending per pupil across the regions, which suggest that the levels of expenditure per pupil in

## Diagram 27. **EDUCATION SPENDING**

### 1991 figures

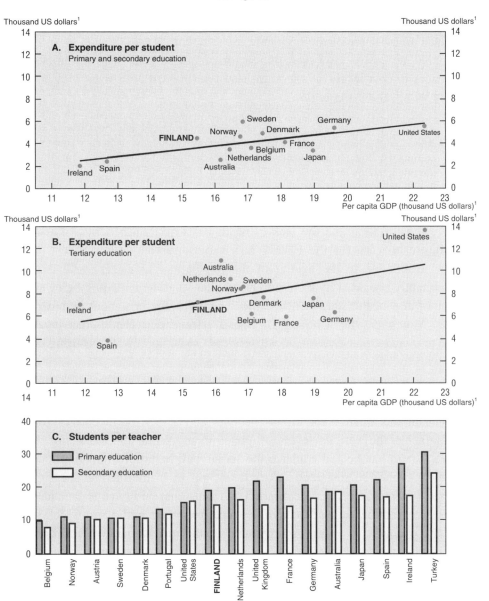

1. In current PPPs.
*Source: Statistical Yearbook of Finland;* OECD, *Education at a Glance,* 1993.

the most expensive regions may not be entirely justified.[54] As transportation costs for pupils (normally paid for by the schools) tend to push up unit costs in sparsely populated regions (like Lappi in the North), while reducing them in more densely populated areas, some of the regional cost differentials may be due to variations in population density. However, this factor cannot be held fully accountable for differences in cost levels, as there are also unexplained cost disparities between schools within the same region.[55]

The fact that *social services and family allowances* constituted one of the most rapidly growing areas of public expenditure during the 1980s and early 1990s is mainly due to an explosion in the demand for day care facilities for young children (0 to 7 years), which cannot be justified by an increase in the number of children in this age group, nor by a rise in the rate of female labour-market participation (Table 25). This development has been greatly facilitated by massive subsidisation and the lack of means tests on cash benefits.[56] Growth in expenditure on care for the elderly has been somewhat more modest, and is largely attributable to the ageing of the population. However, with day care predominantly provided by local public suppliers and their funding being similar to that of the health care centres, the incentives for cost control have been limited. Moreover, the Ministry of Social Affairs and Health has invariably tended to increase standards in social services, while not always ensuring consistency with overall cost-containment objectives.

*In summary*, the Finnish welfare system has shown a tendency to become more expensive over time, reflecting both the relatively easy conditions under which claimants qualify for aid or benefits and a lack of incentives for cost control facing the various levels of government. While the expansion of the welfare system has helped enhance the social well-being of Finnish citizens, its generosity cannot be sustained. Work disincentives in the income security programmes (unemployment compensation and pensions) will have to be addressed, as these programmes appear to have deviated from their initial aim which was to assist those unable to work. An overhaul of the management of local welfare services also needs consideration, notably with a view to increasing cost-efficiency, as well as budgetary planning procedures at the central government level. The following section considers what policy actions have been and might be taken to achieve this.

Table 25.  **Family support and care for the elderly**

Annual average rates of growth, constant prices

|  | | 1980-85 | 1985-91 |
|---|---|---|---|
| **Family support** | | | |
| Social services | | 9.4 | 10.0 |
| Cash benefits | | 9.6 | 5.5 |
| Total | | 9.5 | 7.0 |
| *of which due to growth in:* | | | |
| Child population | | –0.3 | 0.3 |
| Spending per child | | 9.8 | 6.7 |
| **Care for the elderly** | | | |
| Total | | 8.9 | 5.4 |
| *of which due to growth in:* | | | |
| Old age population | | 1.4 | 1.7 |
| Spending per old age person | | 7.5 | 3.7 |
|  | 1980 | 1985 | 1991 |
|  | Per cent of GDP | | |
| *Memorandum items:* | | | |
| Family support, total expenditure | 2.6 | 3.5 | 4.7 |
| Care for the elderly, total expenditure | 0.5 | 0.7 | 0.9 |

*Source:* OECD, Social Security data base and OECD estimates.

# Reforming the system

## *Recent initiatives*

A number of reforms have been recently adopted or planned covering all welfare expenditure programmes including unemployment compensation, pensions, health care, education and social services. These seek to contain the growing cost of the welfare system and make it more efficient. The principle behind those measures implemented in the area of *unemployment compensation* has been to provide greater incentives for unemployed to find and accept employment. The limitation of the benefit period in the basic flat-rate of UA scheme in 1994 is an important step in this direction. Moreover, UA has been brought into line with the eligibility requirements and duration of the UI earnings-related supplementary benefit, which has improved the transparency of the system.

Another measure has been the removal of the government's employment commitment in 1992, which was imposed by the Employment Act in 1987.[57] A restructuring of the financial base of unemployment insurance was also implemented in 1993, by shifting a larger proportion of contributions to employees and reducing that of employers, with a view to containing the amount of non-wage labour costs.

In the area of *pensions*, the most significant measures adopted in the last two years have been the lowering of public-sector pension benefits to levels in the private sector and modifications to pension laws. Effective in 1994, the minimum age for early disability retirement has been raised from 55 to 58 years. This measure will not affect those who are presently 55 or older, however; the right to immediate retirement is maintained for all persons born in 1939 and earlier, while those born in 1940 will be entitled to early retirement in 1998. The minimum age for being entitled to an unemployment pension was raised in several steps after 1989 from 55 to 60 years, and other eligibility requirements have been tightened as well with effect from 1994. In addition, in 1993 the old-age retirement age for public sector workers was raised from 63 to 65 years, the same as in the private sector. The government has been considering reducing the basic amount granted by the National Pension System for those receiving substantial occupational pensions. On the financing side revenue raising measures include an employment tax and mandatory pensions contributions for wage earners.

As indicated above, the old *grant system*, which involved *ex post* reimbursement of the cost of local welfare services, was abolished in January 1993. Grant allocations to municipalities are now fixed in advance without being earmarked for specific services. However, although the system will gradually evolve to one in which the allocations are fixed according to demographic, geographic, health and financial criteria, at present the grants are still predominantly based upon historical costs. Once fully phased in by the year 2000, the new system will have two main advantages. *First*, it will encourage cost consciousness at the local level, as increased local expenditure no longer triggers additional funding from the state. *Second*, it will considerably facilitate the control of central government expenditure, as the benchmark variables on which the grants are based, even in a medium-term perspective, are known well in advance with only a minor margin of error. In addition to this change in nature, grants and associated local expenditure have been cut by large amounts in recent years to respect the medium-term budgetary framework. Since 1991, various cuts in the number of staff of local public services have been implemented, and employment in this area is expected to fall by 10 per cent by 1997.

In the field of *health care*, the new grant system potentially removes an important source of misallocation of resources, as the system of automatic cost reimbursement of hospitals and health centres is replaced by fixed budgets. Moreover, as a complement to the new grant system, health centres and hospitals now have to negotiate with the municipalities on the allocation of the available resources, and experiments are being carried out with payments by municipalities to hospitals based on invoices specifying the actual treatment per patient.[58] Finally, service fees charged by the medical institutions have been allowed to rise, strengthening the link between contributions and consumption of health-care services.[59] However, incentives for municipalities to avoid referral of patients to institutions in other communities have not been eliminated.

Concerns about cost-efficiency in primary and secondary schooling have also been reflected in the design of a new grant system for *education*. The aim of this reform is to improve educational standards at reduced costs through enhanced competition between providers of the same type of education. To this effect: *i)* support to state-owned institutions and to the municipalities will be made dependent upon objective criteria, such as student numbers and national average cost levels; *ii)* local governments are henceforth obliged to cover educational expenses for students choosing senior secondary or vocational education in other parts of the country; and *iii)* the choice of comprehensive schools has been extended to establishments outside the school district of residence, though parents are responsible for any additional transportation costs. Moreover, the government intends to make the secondary schools system more market oriented by giving direct financial aid to students to pay for transport and accommodation, in contrast with the present system where population density determines a part of per pupil grants.

As regards higher education, the authorities had already in the late 1980s acknowledged the need for a shift in focus from expansion – the number of university graduates and teaching staff rose by, respectively, 100 and 190 per cent from 1960 to 1985 – to enhanced quality and better resource control. This reflected the recognition that the number of students dropping out was rising and that there was an apparent mismatch between supply and demand on the labour market, with students graduating from humanities and social sciences experiencing difficulties finding appropriate jobs. In this context, a reform process focusing on more "result-oriented" appropriation criteria was started in 1986. In particular, the intention was to move from funding related to the number of students to one based, *inter alia*, on the number of degrees secured. At the same time, educational institutions obtained greater discretionary power and a simpler executive structure. However, some of these reforms were overtaken by events in the 1990s, when the economic crisis sparked off a range of expenditure cuts.[60] One salient example was the cut in grants designed to reward educational institutions with an above-average cost-efficiency. As that arrangement only applied to the allocation of *increases* in funds, it lost its effectiveness when grants were reduced rather than raised.

## *The need for further action*

As suggested by the Secretariat's simulations based on the calculations of the Committee on Social Expenditure discussed above, the reforms of the welfare system implemented so far are insufficient to contain the rising trends in welfare expenditure and its adverse implications for overall government spending and public finances. Reductions in unemployment expenditure would require efforts in a number of areas, including eligibility criteria, benefit durations and benefit levels. Better co-ordination of the systems of unemployment compensation and old-age income replacement would be necessary in order to eliminate incentives for early retirement. More generally, the pension system would need to be reviewed in order to make it actuarially sound through reducing the uncovered liabilities (see Part II). There also appears to be scope for a reduction in local government spending through improved efficiency in the fields of education, health care and social services. Finally, budgetary procedures should be redesigned in order to facilitate the implementation of these measures.

### *Adjusting income security programmes*

The debt dynamics discussed above not only shed light on the severity of Finland's welfare spending problems but also reveal their dual nature. *First*, the combination of high unemployment coupled with the generous system of income security has contributed to excessive public expenditure and government debt in the early 1990s, a trend which, under unchanged policies, is likely to persist during the rest of the decade. *Second*, with the population ageing the generous retirement benefits and entitlements to publicly provided health-care and social services will create substantial pressure on welfare spending in the future, which the government may have difficulties financing.

The report by the Finnish Committee on Social Expenditure provides some valuable insights into how these problems could be addressed.[61] To start with, the current unemployment compensation system should swiftly be redesigned in order to remove the web of built-in, unintended work disincentives which has become apparent in recent years. This could be established through *i)* limiting the benefit duration of UI to, for example, 160 days; *ii)* removing the child supplement for unemployed; and *iii)* lengthening the period of employment required for eligibility. Such changes would lower total payments of unemployment compensation by decreasing the number of beneficiaries while maintaining an effective system consistent with the intentions of its original designers – *i.e.* a social insurance system which provides temporary income replacement to active job seekers.

To cope with future liabilities on the pension front, these measures could be supplemented by a rise in the legal retirement age. This could be coupled with either a further increase of the minimum age for early retirement (including the unemployment and ‘‘early’’ invalidity pensions) or a decrease in relative benefits associated with it. Calculations by the Finnish Committee suggest that such measures, in combination with further cuts in health care and social services expenditure, could reduce future social spending by around $2^{1}/_{2}$ and $6^{1}/_{2}$ per cent of GDP in 2000 and 2030 respectively. Such a reduction could have a significant impact on public debt developments. According to Secretariat estimates, it would allow gross debt to fall in the first decade of the next century to around 40 per cent in 2010, a level broadly sustainable in the following decades (Table 26 and Diagram 28).[62] If, on the other hand, the initial reduction in social expenditure by the end of this decade were not followed by further cuts early in the next century, demographic developments would lead to an unsustainable debt accumulation. This illustrates the necessity of reducing entitlements beyond the medium term.

### Enhancing cost-efficiency

The reform of the grant system, in conjunction with changes in the regulatory framework, should have a favourable impact on the cost-efficiency of local

Table 26.   **Public finance scenarios**[1]

Per cent of GDP

|  | 1993 | 1995 | 2000 | 2010 | 2020 | 2030 |
|---|---|---|---|---|---|---|
| **Scenario I:** | | | | | | |
| *"Unchanged welfare policy"* | | | | | | |
| Primary balance[2] | −7.6 | −3.9 | 0.5 | 0.6 | −4.7 | −9.7 |
| Net interest receipts | 0.5 | −1.2 | −3.1 | −2.4 | −6.0 | −15.9 |
| Net lending | −7.1 | −5.1 | −2.6 | −1.8 | −10.7 | −25.6 |
| Gross debt[3] | 62.0 | 80.0 | 95.0 | 98.0 | 148.0 | 282.0 |
| **Scenario II:** | | | | | | |
| *Welfare expenditure cuts of 2¹/₂ per cent* | | | | | | |
| *of GDP in 2000, increasing up to 6¹/₂ per* | | | | | | |
| *cent in 2030 relative* | | | | | | |
| *to the "unchanged welfare policy"* | | | | | | |
| *scenario* | | | | | | |
| Primary balance[2] | −7.6 | −3.9 | 3.0 | 4.1 | 0.8 | −3.2 |
| Net interest receipts | 0.5 | −1.2 | −2.5 | 0.9 | 2.9 | 2.8 |
| Net lending | −7.1 | −5.1 | 0.5 | 5.0 | 3.7 | −0.4 |
| Gross debt[3] | 62.0 | 80.0 | 87.0 | 52.0 | 27.0 | 30.0 |
| **Scenario III:** | | | | | | |
| *Welfare expenditure cut by 2¹/₂ per cent* | | | | | | |
| *of GDP in 2000-2030 relative* | | | | | | |
| *to the "unchanged welfare policy"* | | | | | | |
| *scenario* | | | | | | |
| Primary balance[2] | −7.6 | −3.9 | 3.0 | 3.1 | −2.2 | −7.2 |
| Net interest receipts | 0.5 | −1.2 | −2.5 | 0.5 | 0.7 | −3.7 |
| Net lending | −7.1 | −5.1 | 0.5 | 3.6 | −1.5 | −10.9 |
| Gross debt[3] | 62.0 | 80.0 | 87.0 | 58.0 | 58.0 | 120.0 |

|  | 1980-1990 | 1990-1995 | 1995-2000 | 2000-2010 | 2010-2020 | 2020-2030 |
|---|---|---|---|---|---|---|
| **Underlying macroeconomic projections**[4] | | | | | | |
| Annual average GDP growth | 3.2 | −1.8 | 4 | 3 | 1¹/₂ | 1¹/₂ |
| Contribution from: | | | | | | |
| Fall in the unemployment rate | 0.1 | −3.2 | 1 | 1 | 0 | 0 |
| Growth in labour force | 0.5 | −0.5 | ¹/₂ | 0 | −¹/₂ | −¹/₂ |
| Increase in labour productivity | 2.6 | 1.9 | 2¹/₂ | 2 | 2 | 2 |

1.   Tax/GDP ratio kept constant at its projected 1995 level throughout the projection period.
2.   General goverment net lending less net interest receipts.
3.   In all projections, gross assets as a percentage of GDP is kept at its projected 1995 level of roughly 70 per cent of GDP.
4.   Real long term interest rate projected at 5¹/₂ per cent.
*Source:* OECD estimates, based upon Social Security projections from Ministry of Social Affairs and Health.

Diagram 28. **ALTERNATIVE WELFARE SCENARIOS
AND LONG-TERM DEBT PROJECTIONS**
Per cent of GDP

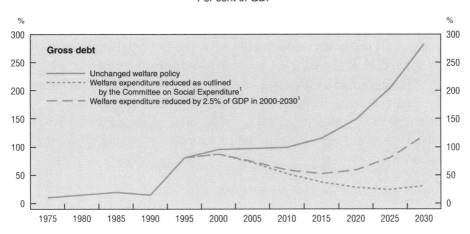

1. See main text.
*Source:* OECD estimates.

government welfare programmes and the associated expenditure. The pursuit of such policies for the education system, building upon the principles of expanded school choice, could help improve quality of education despite tighter budget constraints. As regards the provision of health care, a successful evolution will be conditional on the local government's ability to develop a suitable structure for this sector. In this respect, the reforms enacted to date seem to lag behind developments in some other countries.[63] Future reform efforts in Finland should build on the experience in other countries by increasing the sophistication of the health-purchasing role of public authorities and by enhancing the role played in cost control by primary care doctors.[64] Since it is not obvious that the (450) municipalities are the appropriate administrative framework for health planning, a greater involvement of the central government in orchestrating such reforms may be required.

There may be scope also for additional measures to improve efficiency of and contain expenditure on public services and cash benefits. For example, the state could foster competition in the provision of social services by obliging municipalities to support private suppliers on an equal footing with public ones offering equivalent products, in particular in areas like child care and retirement homes. In addition, the state could further dissociate itself from the micro-management of local services, and relax the standards set by the central government which are, in certain cases, perceived as preventing effective management of such services.[65] A cap on local tax rates is also worth exploring, as it would impose a budget constraint on lower levels of government, adding an incentive to contain local spending. However, while the extension of means tests in family support programmes could be useful as well, forms of means testing which tend to reduce work incentives, notwithstanding a direct cost saving effect, should be approached with caution.[66]

### Redesigning the budget framework

Finally, a number of shortcomings of public sector budgetary procedures should be resolved in order to facilitate a reform of the welfare state. Most prominent among them is, as argued above, the lack of political commitment of the Parliament to the medium-term budgetary framework, limiting both its effectiveness and credibility. It would be desirable for the new government to commit Parliament, or at least the coalition parties that constitute the government, to medium-term ceilings for individual spending programmes, notably in the welfare area. The present practice of largely equiproportionate cuts in all types of spending to reach overall expenditure targets is unlikely to yield a rational composition of public spending. It would also be advisable to start rather than end the budget cycle with a vote on expenditure ceilings, which – once output developments stabilise – could perhaps best be formulated in cyclically-adjusted terms to help assess the structural position of government finances. Under present circumstances of very tight budgeting, the government could also request that parliamentary proposals for (discretionary) spending increases be offset by proposed savings of equivalent size; to this end, an attempt should be made to restrict by law the number of supplementary budget bills during the execution of a budget.

# IV. Conclusions

After three years of deep recession – marked by a total drop in output of about 15 per cent – the Finnish economy is now recovering. For the first time since 1990, GDP growth turned positive in the second half of 1993 and, for 1994 as a whole, is estimated to reach 3½ per cent in real terms. As a result, there has been a modest decline in the unemployment rate from its peak of 19 per cent in early 1994, while inflation has remained low, at around 2 per cent. Together with a significant improvement in the external position, these developments have contributed to strengthen the exchange rate, thereby reducing the overall depreciation of the currency against the Ecu, since October 1991, to 18 per cent.

So far, the upswing appears to have been mainly driven by a strong surge in exports, reflecting the substantial competitiveness gains associated with the fall in the markka and moderate development of wage costs. However, evidence of a slight pickup of domestic demand has emerged recently. Supported by easier monetary conditions and an improved household financial position, consumer confidence is strengthening somewhat, which is reflected in increased purchases of durable goods. Manufacturing investment is also rising, following a return to more normal levels of capacity utilisation and stronger corporate profitability in export industries. But, given the continued weakness of non-manufacturing and housing investment, a significant imbalance still persists between the rapidly expanding open sector of the economy and the sluggish domestic-oriented industries.

Current OECD projections suggest an acceleration of the recovery in the next two years, with real GDP growth approaching 4¾ per cent in 1995 before stabilising at around 4 per cent in 1996. The upturn is also expected to become more broadly based, spreading from exports to household demand and business investment. Indeed, with the private sector's financial consolidation process apparently coming to an end, and improved confidence associated with Finland's accession to the European Union, both personal consumption and spending on machinery and equipment should show more robust growth. This is projected to lead to a further reduction in unemployment, but, given continued slack in the labour market, wage and price inflation is expected to remain subdued. At the same time, helped by sustained exports and favourable terms of trade, the improvement in the external balance should consolidate further, with the current account surplus projected to reach 3 per cent of GDP in 1995.

Uncertainty still prevails, however, as to whether the revival of domestic demand will be strong enough to keep the economy growing. There is concern, in particular, that the recent increases in long-term interest rates, which have been more pronounced in Finland than in many other OECD countries, may hurt the nascent recovery of investment. Another uncertainty relates to wage and price behaviour during the current upswing. With employment prospects improving, wage pressure could develop in the export manufacturing industries and, as a result of collective wage bargaining, spill over to the rest of the economy. Consequently, there is a risk that domestic inflation may prove stronger than assumed in the projections.

In this context, with the economy gathering momentum, the priority for policy-makers should be to strengthen fiscal discipline in order to consolidate the budget situation further. Given the high tax burden already prevailing in the country, emphasis in this regard should be on spending restraint rather than on tax increases. The austerity measures taken so far, which have focused on curbing government consumption and investment, have resulted in some improvement of the general government budget position. From its peak – 7 per cent of GDP – reached in 1993, the general government deficit has declined to around 5 per cent of GDP in 1994 and is expected to remain approximately at that level in 1995. Such progress in restoring control over government finances appears even more significant when adjustment is made for the budgetary cost of EU accession (notably the increased income support to farmers, to compensate for a drop in agricultural prices) and the temporary impact of tax refunds. These factors will indeed adversely affect the 1995 central government deficit, which is projected to stay at the same level (10 per cent of GDP) as in the two previous years.

Despite the corrective actions on government spending, the gross public debt – which, at 70 per cent of GDP, already exceeds the OECD average – is set to continue to rise in 1995. Such prospects may raise concerns in financial markets, making the economy vulnerable to changes in international investors' sentiment, as evidenced by the recent widening of long-term interest rate differentials with Germany. The debt outlook appears all the more difficult since the rising cost of the welfare system – which currently absorbs almost 75 per cent of general government non-interest spending – will tend to put heavy pressure on public finances in the coming decades, due, mainly, to a rapidly-ageing population.

Against this background, therefore, it is crucial that the present fiscal objective of limiting the volume of central government expenditure to its 1991 level by 1995, with the exclusion of spending related to EU accession and bank support operations, be achieved. A reformulation of the medium-term budgetary framework, to make it more transparent and more binding, would also be desirable for the years to come. This would require that the announced expenditure ceilings be articulated within the framework of a clear path of deficit-reduction targets, consistent with a gradual decline in the public debt/GDP ratio over time. Another improvement would be to give the spending limits greater force by making them subject to parliamentary approval; this would facilitate the enforcement of expenditure savings in areas – such as welfare spending – where a large majority in Parliament is usually needed.

Additional progress in fiscal consolidation would ease the future operation of monetary policy. With continued weak inflation pressure over the last eighteen months, the monetary authorities have been able to reduce short-term interest rates gradually to levels prevailing elsewhere in Europe. Since the floating of the currency in September 1992, money market rates have declined from $16\frac{1}{2}$ per cent to 5 per cent. By contrast, after falling substantially until February 1994, long-term interest rates have risen progressively since then (from $6\frac{1}{2}$ to around 10 per cent). As a result, *real* bond yields are now about 5 per cent above their average value in the 1980s. Such a high risk premium built into Finnish long rates prevents the economy from fully reaping the benefits of a low inflation environment. Hence, as argued above, the necessity for a more rapid reduction of government deficits and debt in order to relieve the pressure in financial markets while activity gains strength.

Continued success in keeping inflation under control would also contribute to maintain low interest rates as this would give the monetary authorities the credibility needed to influence positively market expectations. The ability of the central bank to meet the announced inflation target of 2 per cent from 1995 onwards will be important in this regard. As the impressive price performance observed in recent years, particularly in view of the significant depreciation of the currency, coincided with a depressed output and employment environment, it is unclear to what extent monetary policy has regained credibility since the implementation of the inflation target. This approach to policy will thus be more fully tested during the emerging recovery.

Given the constraints bearing on the conduct of monetary and fiscal policies, structural reform will be the key to foster growth in the medium term. Following the major reforms introduced in the late 1980s in the fields of taxation, competition policy, the public sector and pensions, structural initiatives have focused mainly on preparing the ground for a full participation in the European integration process. Most have been related to the implementation of the European Economic Area Agreement and the accession to the European Union (EU). In this context, measures have been adopted recently to adjust the system of indirect taxation towards an EU-type of value-added tax and to make farm support consistent with EU common agricultural policies. In addition, a substantial privatisation programme (involving eleven state companies) has been launched, supplemented by a deregulation of the telecommunication market. Also, with bank profitability improving slightly, government policies towards banking have moved away from crisis management, through direct support to the banks, to actions designed to strengthen the restructuring and supervision of the banking industry. Finally, in order to enhance labour-market flexibility, the government has supported shifts towards a more decentralised wage formation process at the sectoral level. At the same time, restrictions on private placement services have been lifted.

Further progress could be envisaged in some of these areas, however. Concerning agriculture, in particular, the level of subsidies has remained high by international standards, with market price support accounting for as much as four-fifths of total assistance to farmers and food industries. Given the misallocation of resources induced by the existing support scheme, and its drawbacks for consumers, a reduction of protection in this sector would bring substantial welfare gains. Moreover, the scope of the privatisation programme could be widened, so as to include public companies in the transportation and communication industries. Attempts to rationalise the size of the banking sector should also be encouraged in order to scale down banks' operating costs – the highest among Nordic countries – and promote a leaner and more efficient financial system. Furthermore, additional action would be needed to improve the functioning of the labour market in order to increase employment opportunities for new entrants and facilitate the reinsertion of the unemployed. Important in this regard would be the implementation of more effective active labour-market measures to provide the unemployed with the skills currently required in the export sector. Other measures affecting wage setting should also be considered, including the removal of the minimum wage clauses for non-unionised workers, the relaxation of restrictions on fixed-term contracts, and, more generally, the reduction of taxation on wages.

As discussed in detail in Part III of the Survey, there is also considerable scope for reforming the welfare system, with a view to both containing the rapid growth of public expenditure and removing the labour market distortions generated by the system. A key feature of the Finnish welfare state is its universality; all citizens are entitled to publicly-provided income security (including generous unemployment benefits and retirement pensions), health care, education and social services. The duration of unemployment benefits is relatively long – more than two years – and the effective rates of income replacement high by international standards. The pension scheme offers universal coverage for invalidity and early retirement, with the latter also open to the unemployed. The provision of health care, education and social services is predominantly ensured by local governments, with user charges typically covering only a small fraction of the total costs involved. As a result, despite municipalities having a relatively large tax autonomy, they also receive significant transfers (''grants'') from the central government. In addition to the above-mentioned welfare programmes, there is an extensive regime of ''cash benefits'' – including rent subsidies, child support, maternity leave allowances, etc. – administered by the national security system.

Given these characteristics, as in other Nordic countries, the Finnish welfare system has been relatively successful in achieving government social objectives, but it has also become very costly. Indeed, after steadily increasing as a share of GDP during the 1980s, welfare expenditure rose dramatically in the wake of the sharp recession of the early 1990s. Moreover, as noted, the ageing of the population is expected to give a further boost to welfare spending – particularly on pensions, health care and social services. The adverse consequences of such demographic developments are set to surface as early as in the next decade, when the post-war "baby boom" generation becomes eligible for early retirement programmes.

While such a rising burden of the system has, to a large extent, been the reflection of its combined universality and generosity, it is also the result of a number of problems inherent in the functioning of the system. *First,* due to weak eligibility requirements, welfare programmes – such as disability and early retirement – currently enrol a large number of qualified workers, either employed or unemployed, for whom they were not originally designed. *Second,* many beneficiaries of the unemployment compensation scheme – whose entitlements are based on earnings prevailing before the recession – receive an income higher than they could now earn in the labour market. This tends to create work disincentives through welfare dependency. *Third,* the lack of incentives to control spending has greatly contributed to the rising cost of health care, education and social services. The "grant system", in particular, has encouraged the provision of local welfare services by municipalities, the more so since these could rely – until very recently – on an almost automatic funding from the state.

To cope with these problems, a number of reforms have recently been introduced. Since January 1994, the indefinite duration for the basic unemployment allowance has been dropped, and the rules governing entitlement to such benefits have been tightened. These measures are intended to provide greater incentives for the unemployed to find jobs. Job seekers who no longer qualify for the unemployment allowance scheme can be enrolled in a new social assistance programme designed to provide support of "last resort". In the area of pensions, the standard retirement age for civil servants was raised in 1993, a decision followed, in 1994, by an increase in the minimum age for early retirement for all categories of workers. Moreover, the grant system was changed in 1993, so as to encourage cost savings at the local level and allow a tighter control of welfare spending by the central government. To this end, grant allocations from the state to municipalities are now fixed in advance, without being earmarked for specific services.

As these reforms will not be sufficient to contain the rapid growth of welfare spending expected in the future, there remains ample scope for improving the cost effectiveness of the various welfare programmes. With respect to unemployment compensation, benefit *durations* could be reduced and eligibility requirements tightened further. Benefit *levels* for both unemployment compensation and early retirement schemes could also be scaled down. In addition, given the projected demographic developments, a general increase in the standard retirement age and in the minimum age for early retirement would seem appropriate. Finally, control over local welfare spending could be strengthened by introducing competition in the provision of social services. More generally, a cap on local taxes would be worth exploring to restrain municipalities' spending.

*In summary,* after its worst recession in post-war history, the Finnish economy is now recovering. Booming exports, helped by a large depreciation of the currency and wage moderation, have been, so far, the main support to activity. With private consumption and investment now responding to the easier monetary conditions and an improved financial environment, the upturn is expected to spread over domestic demand, thus becoming more broadly based. As the recovery gathers momentum, progress in fiscal consolidation appears to be of crucial importance. Additional spending restraint, notably in the area of growing welfare expenditure, will be needed to curb rising government deficits and debt. This would contribute to alleviate interest rate pressure and, together with the maintenance of price stability, help restore monetary policy credibility. Continued emphasis on structural reform is also required to sustain growth in the medium term and reduce the persistently high unemployment. In particular, further initiatives would seem essential both to improve the cost effectiveness of the extensive welfare programmes and lessen the distorting effects of these programmes on the labour market.

# Notes

1. This may partly reflect the 20 percentage-point reduction in the motor vehicle tax effective 12 July 1993.

2. While this change is virtually budgetary neutral, the CPI is raised due to compositional effects.

3. Following SNA practice, in 1993 the mandatory occupational pension system has been included into general government accounts. Consequently, the general government net lending was reduced by some $3^{1}/_{2}$ per cent of GDP in 1993.

4. Moreover, there are risks attached to these assets which may not be appropriately valued. Around 75 per cent of the pension funds' assets consist of promissory notes issued by contributing firms to temporarily withhold their payments to the pension schemes, as currently authorised; see P. Pylkkönen, ''The employment pension scheme and the financial markets'', *Bank of Finland Bulletin*, December 1991, pp. 6-9.

5. Committee proposal for reforming Central Bank legislation, Helsinki 1994.

6. The first phrases of Section 2 of the Draft Act stipulate that ''The objective of the Bank of Finland shall be to safeguard the value of money.''

7. The focus on money market rates is appropriate in the case of Finland, since the lending rates charged by banks and pension institutions, which constitute the main sources of credit, are largely tied to these rates.

8. As originally developed by the Bank of Canada – see C. Freedman, ''The Use of Indicators and Monetary Condition Index in Canada'', *IMF Staff Papers* (forthcoming) – this approach is also used in Norway and Sweden.

9. In fact, it could be argued that overall monetary conditions continued to ease after June 1993, as the fall in short-term interest rates and the exchange rate appreciation (lowering the markka value of foreign loans) had a positive spin-off on private sector balance sheets – an effect not captured by the index.

10. See in this respect two articles entitled ''Economic Development, Inflation and Monetary Policy'' and ''Fiscal Policy and Public Finance'' in the *Economic Bulletin* 6-7 and 8 of the Bank of Finland. Evidence is also provided by the Bank of Norway in *Penge og kreditt* 1994/3.

11. Excluding asset management companies Siltapankki and Arsenal (see below), which have taken over non-performing assets of troubled banks.

12. Again with the exclusion of the performance of asset management companies.

13. According to a survey carried out by the Confederation of Finnish Industries and Employers in June 1994, about half of small firms, 70 per cent of medium-sized firms and 79 per cent of larger firms reported that they did not experience financing problems.

14. This may partly be explained by the fact that, during the recession, banks used to grant new loans to existing customers at rates of interest below their own funding costs, in order to avoid even more costly bankruptcies. With the recovery gathering pace, this practice has largely been discontinued, thus leading to a widening of the differential between the average lending rate and money market rates.

15. A transitional period of five to seven years has been granted for a number of programmes, mainly linked to debt rescheduling and investment subsidies for pig and poultry farming.

16. The Producer Subsidy Equivalent measures the total support given to an industry, including direct subsidies, import quota and tariffs and favourable tax treatment. This support is expressed as a percentage of the total production value.

17. This is a new type of regions, defined within the framework of EU support programmes, established in connection with the accession treaties for the Nordic countries, granting such regions the right to beneficial treatment on par with the regions officially recognised as being the poorest within EU, so-called "goal 6" regions.

18. In particular the broadening of the base for capital income and indirect taxes.

19. A detailed examination of these issues can be found in "The Nordic Banking Crisis", Heikki Koskenkylä, *Bank of Finland Bulletin*, August 1994.

20. The size and mechanisms of such official support to the banks are discussed in the 1992/93 *OECD Economic Survey of Finland*, pp. 37-40.

21. As shown in Table 16, such a guarantee legally materialised in 1994.

22. Established as a part of the banking rescue package in March 1992, with the aim of ensuring the stability of the banking system and to secure the claims of domestic and foreign depositors.

23. Taken over by the Government Guarantee Fund in 1992, see 1992/93 *OECD Economic Survey of Finland*.

24. Peter Nyberg and Vesa Vihriälä, "The Finnish Banking Crisis and Its Handling", *Bank of Finland Discussion Papers*, 94/7. The report uses data that goes up to 1991 inclusive. While the rationalisation efforts since 1991 has lead to further streamlining, that has not been sufficient to affect the conclusion about excessive capacity in a Nordic context.

25. See Aranko, Jorma,"Reorganisation of Financial Market Supervision in Finland", *Bank of Finland Bulletin*, February 1994.

26. This Survey contained a special chapter dealing with labour market institutions and policies. See 1992/93 *OECD Economic Survey of Finland*, pp. 50-67.

27. For instance, the May 1993 agreement between employer organisations and unions, which allowed firms to pay young workers less than the minimum wage during the first twelve months after recruitment, could be made permanent and perhaps extended to other groups particularly exposed to unemployment.

28.  OECD *Jobs Study*, Part II, "The Adjustment Potential of the Labour Market", OECD, 1994.

29.  See OECD *Jobs Study*, 1994, *op. cit.*

30.  A full description of the system can be found in *Functioning of the Unemployment security system in Finland*, by Pertti Tuhkanen, Ministry of Finance, February 1994 (mimeographed).

31.  Mk 24 for one child, Mk 34 for two and Mk 44 for three or more children.

32.  The earnings-related amount plus child supplement cannot exceed 90 per cent of the daily pay insured.

33.  The amount of the spouse's income exceeding Mk 300 per month (excluding child allowances) is taken into account.

34.  The Finnish pension scheme was discussed extensively in the 1991/92 *OECD Economic Survey of Finland*. For detailed institutional information, see also The Central Pension Security Institute, Statistical Yearbook of pensioners in Finland, Helsinki, 1992.

35.  The annual index adjustment of the occupational pensions is based on the arithmetic average of changes in both earnings and the consumer price index (the so-called TEL index).

36.  See Part II; the remainder is invested in government bonds, shares and real estate.

37.  Following SNA practice, these privately managed, but mandatory pension schemes have been integrated into the general government accounts. See Part II.

38.  These range in size from Helsinki – with about a half a million people – to very small communities with less than a thousand people.

39.  OECD, *Education at a glance: OECD Indicators*, Paris, 1993.

40.  In practice, however, given significant differences between countries in the definition and set-up of government spending programmes, strict comparison of expenditure levels is rather difficult.

41.  See *Sosiaalimenotoimikunnan Mietintö*, Ministry of Social Affairs and Health, Helsinki, September 1994. The projections exclude expenditure on education.

42.  Expenditure projections for items constituting two-thirds of total non-interest expenditure in 1993 come from the report referred to above. The remaining spending components, essentially subsidies, education and "public goods", have been projected by the OECD Secretariat. However, underlying assumptions about growth of labour force, employment, labour productivity and GDP are taken straight from the report's most optimistic growth scenario.

43.  The present funding rules of the social security system would automatically trigger higher contribution rates from employees, employers and public authorities, thus leading to a higher tax share of GDP, as social security contributions are included in the total tax take. In this sense, the extrapolations presented do not embody – in a technical sense – unchanged policies, but assume that an increase in social security contributions is offset by a fall in other taxes.

44.  In the preparation of the 1995 Budget, the Cabinet did not even commit itself to the "cheese-slicing" based expenditure ceilings, but only agreed to an overall expenditure ceiling.

45.  Neither was there a firm basis for imposing any sanctions, as the agreements were framed in terms of total local government expenditure.

46. Around 80 per cent of claims for housing support come from the unemployed.

47. This trend stopped in 1992 when per capita expenditure in health care fell by 3.7 per cent.

48. See OECD, *Progress in Structural Reform, an overview*, Paris, 1992.

49. However, before the grant reform, new posts had to be approved by provincial boards which allowed demographic considerations to determine the allocation of these posts.

50. Investment is covered by a separate programme funded by municipalities and the state.

51. A. Iivari and R. Jämsén, *Inter-municipal variations in social and health care expenditure in 1989*, Ministry of Social Affairs and Health, Department for Research and Development, Helsinki, 1992; R. Laamanen, *The use of health center hospitals and its regional variation in Finland*, Department of General Practice and Primary Health Care, University of Helsinki, Finland, November 1992.

52. A compensating system of transfers could be put in place with a view to offsetting the equity effects of user charging. Such an approach, though, would entail significant administrative and monitoring costs.

53. See OECD, *Education in OECD Countries: A Compendium of Statistical information*, Paris, 1993.

54. A recent study suggest that vocational and senior secondary schools have even higher differences in per pupil expenditure than the comprehensive school system, see Government Institute for Economic Research (VATT), *Koulutuksen suoritekohtaisten käyttömenojen eroista*, Helsinki, 1991.

55. For example, average differentials of the cost per pupil between individual schools within the three most populous regions are in the order of 15 to 22 per cent. Neither can the large cost differentials be attributed to differences in quality of teaching, as there appears to be only a very weak correlation between spending per pupil and performance in test scores. See Government Institute for Economic Research (VATT), *Ollin oppivuosi 13 000 – 56 000 markkaa – peruskoulujen oppilaskohtaisten kustannuserojen ekonometrinen analyysi*, Helsinki, 1992.

56. Parents' own contributions as a percentage of total costs were on average 10 per cent in 1990, the lowest among the Nordic countries. User charges for day care institutions are progressive.

57. This Act committed central and local governments to providing either a temporary job or training for young and long-term unemployed (after an unemployment period of three and twelve months, respectively).

58. R. Jämsén and K. Klemola, *OECD's cross national study of hospital financing: the national report of Finland*, Ministry of Social Affairs and Health, Helsinki, 1993; I. Vohlonen, M. Pekurinen, P. Paunio, *Contractual Management of Municipal Health Care in Finland*, Health Services Research Ltd., Helsinki, 1994.

59. In 1993 the contributions by municipalities, state grants and patient fees were 56.5, 36 and 7.5 per cent respectively against 49, 45.4 and 5.6 per cent in 1991.

60. Some positive results have been observed, though, such as lower drop out ratios.

61. Ministry for Social Affairs and Health, *op cit.*

62. A report by the president's Commission on Employment, which appeared on 30 September 1994 and has been approved by the government on 16 November, proposes expenditure cuts amounting to Mk 16 billion by 1999 – roughly the equivalent of $2^1/_2$ per cent of GDP. The proposals include cuts in grants to local authorities and a withholding of index adjustments of public pensions for the years 1993, 1994 and 1995.

63. See, for example, the 1993/94 *OECD Economic Survey of the United Kingdom*, for an extensive analysis of the reforms that have been implemented in this country.

64. This would involve a move away from straightforward fee-for-service payments schemes that have become slightly more important under the reforms.

65. In particular within social services and primary education, standards defining personnel norms and professional qualifications are seen as excessively detailed. In 1994, the Association of Municipalities presented a report which addresses these issues.

66. For example, enhanced means testing within the National Pension System – as suggested by the Government – would enlarge the effective marginal tax rate, thus reducing the incentives to work and save.

*Annex*

# Chronology of main economic events and policy measures

## 1992

### September

On 8 September, the Bank of Finland decides to temporarily float the markka. The decision is taken with the consent of the government in accordance with the Currency Act.

Parliament passes a law by which a specified minority (at least one-third) of the members of parliament will no longer be empowered to veto spending reductions except for measures aiming at cutting basic social security benefits.

The government submits its 1993 budget to Parliament. The net financing requirement is projected to be Mk 48 billion (9.2 per cent of GDP).

### October

The Bank of Finland raises the banks' cash reserve requirement from 3.7 to 4 per cent of the cash reserve base.

The government decides expenditure cuts amounting to Mk 8.5 billion for 1993, Mk 16 billion for 1994 and Mk 20 billion for 1995.

### November

The Currency Act is amended so as to enable the government to authorise the Bank of Finland to abandon the limits on the markka's fluctuation range for an indefinite period. However, the government can cancel such authorisation, after taking into consideration the conditions prevailing in the money and foreign exchange markets. Prior to making the decision, the government must request the opinion of the Bank of Finland on the matter.

On 13 November, the government, in accordance with the amended Currency Act, decides to authorise the Bank of Finland to prolong the floating of the markka.

The Bank of Finland raises the banks' cash reserve requirement from 4 to 4.5 per cent of the cash reserve base.

Labour market partners agree to extend the wage agreement of November 1991. As a consequence, no contractual wage increases are granted for 1993. If the rise in the consumer price index exceeds 3.9 per cent between October 1992 and September 1993, wages and salaries will be raised by the same amount as the price overshooting. The government and the employee organisations agree that the government cancels its bill proposing changes in the unemployment insurance scheme.

## December

The Government Guarantee Fund decides to grant capital support totalling Mk 1.5 billion to Skopbank and Mk 4.7 billion to the Savings Bank of Finland.

The Bank of Finland raises the banks' cash reserve requirement from 4.5 to 5 per cent of the cash reserve base.

## 1993

## January

The Parliamentary Supervisory Board lowers the Bank of Finland's base rate from 9.5 to 8.5 per cent.

The Bank of Finland raises the banks' cash reserve requirement from 5 to 5.5 per cent of the cash reserve base. It also decides to lower the rate of interest paid on cash reserve deposits. The new interest rate will be 3 percentage points below the three-month Helibor, but not less than 8 per cent.

The Nordic central banks decide to revise and substantially widen their agreement on short-term currency support, in force since 1984.

The 1939 Restriction Act is repealed and replaced by new legislation lifting the restrictions on foreign ownership of Finnish companies. This new legislation also liberalises the acquisition of real estate by foreigners.

A new capital income (gains) tax is introduced. Individual capital gains will be taxed at a flat rate of 25 per cent. The corporate tax rate will be 25 per cent as well.

The government decides to raise a (progressively determined) "compulsory loan" in connection with the withholding tax on personal income. Contributions to the loan range from 2 to 4 per cent of taxable income in excess of Mk 100 000.

The government extends the operations of the Regional Development Fund to the whole country.

New entrants to the labour force must wait three months to qualify for unemployment benefits, instead of six weeks.

Local governments' obligation to provide a job or education for young and long-term unemployed, according to the Employment Act, is cancelled.

The central government budget for 1993 is approved by Parliament. Net borrowing requirement amounts to Mk 45 billion (9.1 per cent of GDP).

## February

The Bank of Finland specifies the guidelines for monetary policy over the next few years. The aim is to stabilise the annual rate of inflation at 2 per cent by 1995. Inflation is measured by the consumer price index, adjusted for public charges, taxes and changes in capital cost of housing.

The Parliamentary Supervisory Board lowers the Bank of Finland's base rate from 8.5 to 7.5 per cent.

The Parliament unanimously approves a resolution requiring the Finnish state to guarantee that Finnish banks meet their commitments under all circumstances. At the same time, the Parliament undertakes to grant the government whatever funds and powers might be necessary for this purpose.

Finland starts negotiations with the European Community for possible membership.

The Parliament approves the first supplementary budget for 1993. Mk 15 billion additional resources are authorised for supporting the banking sector. The net borrowing requirement is increased to Mk 60.4 billion.

## March

The following changes are introduced in the organisation of the Government Guarantee Fund: the board of management includes five members, at least one of whom represents the Ministry of Finance; the Parliamentary Supervisory body continues to function as the Fund's supervisory body and appoints the members of the board; a full-time Fund's manager, assisted by permanent staff, is appointed; the Fund assists the Ministry of Finance in the preparation of decisions concerning the use of resources earmarked for bank support in the state budget; support measures by the Fund must be approved by the government.

The Parliament approves the second supplementary budget for 1993, increasing spending by Mk 1.7 billion to support private investment.

The government endorses the inflation targeting announced in February by the Bank of Finland.

The budgetary framework for spending and personnel is determined for 1994 and 1995, and submitted to the ministries in conjunction with development of the 1994 budget proposal and the medium-term spending plan for 1994-97.

## April

The Parliament authorises additional borrowing to finance the third supplementary budget to be adopted in July (see below).

The Bank of Finland lowers the banks' cash reserve requirement from 5.5 to 4.5 per cent of the cash reserve base.

The Government Guarantee Fund grants capital support totalling Mk 1.1 billion to the Savings Bank of Finland.

## May

The Parliamentary Supervisory Board lowers the Bank of Finland's base rate from 7.5 to 7 per cent.

Social partners agree that minimum wage provisions might in certain cases be waived for new, young entrants to the labour market with reductions in required pay in the range of 10 to 50 per cent.

The Bank of Finland lowers the banks' cash reserve requirement from 5.5 to 4.5 per cent of the cash reserve base at end-April.

## June

The Bank of Finland lowers the banks' cash reserve requirement from 4.5 to 4 per cent of the cash reserve base and returns the banks' cash reserve deposits on 1 June.

The Bank of Finland announces measures to promote the functioning of the market in government securities by holding weekly repo auctions in government and Bank of Finland securities for the primary dealers.

The President ratifies the protocols and signs the laws concerning the European Economic Area (EEA) agreement.

## July

The Parliamentary Supervisory Board lowers the Bank of Finland's base rate from 7 to 6.5 per cent.

From 1 July, a minimum reserve requirement replaces the previous system of deposits of cash reserves.

The third supplementary budget for 1993 increases state expenditure by Mk 5.9 billion, largely related to unemployment compensation, debt servicing and subsidisation of agricultural exports.

The minimum age for early retirement rises from 55 to 58 years, but remains 55 for those born prior to 1940. The minimum age for part-time retirement is lowered to 58 years from 60, and part-time retirees are not penalised in future pension calculations.

Interest rate subsidies are introduced for households with difficulties servicing mortgages.

The automobile tax is lowered by 20 percentage points.

## August

The Parliamentary Supervisory Board lowers the Bank of Finland's base rate from 6.5 to 6 per cent.

The government guarantees the acquisition of new equity capital by the Union Bank of Finland and Kansallis-Osake-Pankki (KOP) for a total of Mk 2.8 billion.

The government grants Mk 1 billion in capital support to the Savings Bank of Finland, increasing the state's holding in the bank to 99 per cent.

## September

The government submits its 1994 budget to Parliament. The net financing requirement is projected to be Mk 64 billion (12.7 per cent of GDP).

## October

Parliament approves the fourth supplementary budget for 1993.

The government approves the proposal of the Government Guarantee Fund whereby the Savings Bank of Finland is to be sold to its four largest competitor banks.

## November

The government establishes an asset management company called Arsenal Ltd to own and administer the non-performing assets of the Savings Bank of Finland (SBF), which were not included in the parts of the SBF sold in October.

An agreement was reached on state wages and salaries. Part of the bonus holiday pay for 1994 will be accorded as paid holiday and the summer shortening of working hours will be abolished. Cuts in 1994 and 1995 personnel expenditure will be reduced.

## December

The Parliamentary Supervisory Board lowers the Bank of Finland's base rate from 6 to 5.5 per cent.

Parliament approves the fifth supplementary budget for 1993. Incomes and expenditures increase by Mk 6.9 billion.

Parliament approves the 1994 budget. The net borrowing requirement is Mk 68.1 billion (13.5 per cent of GDP).

When making discretionary grants to municipalities, the Ministry of the Interior may set conditions on the use of grants which pertain to the restructuring of the financial position of the municipality concerned.

The government grants capital support to Skopbank by purchasing preferred capital certificates issued by Skopbank for a total value of Mk 350 million.

## 1994

## January

The European Economic Area agreement enters into force.

Thresholds for income tax rates are adjusted by 2 per cent for inflation, and the "compulsory loan" collected from taxpayers through delayed tax refunds is lowered by 1 per cent for incomes between 100 000 and 150 000 Mk/year.

The withholding tax on interest income is raised from 20 to 25 per cent.

The local government tax rate is raised in 124 municipalities and lowered in two.

Pensions are not indexed for inflation in 1994.

Family deductions in income taxation are abandoned in favour of direct income support.

The unemployment insurance premium paid by employers rises from 6 to 6.3 per cent of employers' wage bills.

An energy tax, determined on the basis of energy content, is imposed on all primary sources of energy.

Employment subsidies paid to households in 1994 and 1995 are exempted from taxation.

A new law on business subsidies replaces the law on regional support for business activity. Subsidies now take the forms of investment support for developing regions, small business support and development support for small and medium-sized firms. Business subsidies are directed by a so-called Regional Policy Programme Procedure.

The so-called return lending rate in the pension system is lowered from 7 to 6½ per cent.

## February

The Parliamentary Supervisory Board lowers the Bank of Finland's base rate from 5.5 to 5.25 per cent.

An agreement between timber producers and users determines timber prices for the coming year, effective in March. Average price increases in comparison with 1993 are 14 to 17 per cent.

## March

The Ministry of Finance provides the other ministries with guidelines for expenditures and personnel in the 1995 budget, and publishes a medium-term economic plan for 1995-98.

Parliament approves the first supplementary budget for 1994, increasing spending by Mk 1.7 billion, primarily on infrastructure projects.

## April

The agricultural incomes agreement lowers the guideline price for grains and increases price and production subsidies by Mk 300 million.

## May

A Decision in Principle is made by the Council of State regarding adaptation of Finnish agriculture and regional/structural policy to conform with EU standards. The transition is projected to cost Finland Mk 5.5-6 billion annually.

# June

A new Value-Added Tax Act replaces the Sales Tax Act. Health, social welfare and educational services, as well as financial and insurance services, continue to be tax exempt.

An annual vehicle tax of Mk 300-500/automobile (weighing no more than 3 500 kg) is introduced.

Parliament approves the second supplementary budget for 1994, increasing spending by Mk 1.4 billion primarily on providing education and temporary jobs for youth.

The government reaches a decision in principle that the proportion of state ownership in public industrial and energy companies can be lowered to a significant minority share.

The Treaty of Accession between Finland and the member states of the EU is signed.

# July

In connection with the second supplementary budget for 1994, the state is authorised to borrow an additional Mk 4 billion.

# September

The government submits its 1995 budget to Parliament. The net borrowing requirement is projected to be Mk 61.1 billion (11.3 per cent of GDP).

The government increases the share capital of the asset management company Arsenal Ltd by Mk 6 billion. The capital injection is necessary to cover losses incurred during the year.

The Presidential Commission on Employment submits its report, including proposals for the reduction of the number of unemployed to 200 000 by the year 2000.

# October

In a national referendum, Finland votes to join the European Union by a margin of 57 to 43 per cent.

Parliament approves the third supplementary budget for 1994, increasing spending by Mk 3.3 billion, primarily on unemployment measures, agricultural export subsidies and defense procurement.

The government proposes to abolish the system of primary product discounts in value added taxation. The value added tax on foodstuffs will be 17 per cent during 1995-97, after which it will fall to 12 per cent.


**November**

In 1995 the average rates of employers' (short-term employment) and employees' pension insurance contributions will be 17.8 and 4 per cent of the payroll, respectively.

The Cabinet proposes the implementation of specific recommendations made in the report of the Presidential Commission on Employment, including shifting of expenditure within the budget from pensions and local authorities to employment programmes. Negotiations begin with labour market parties concerning revisions in labour legislation, employee participation funds, unemployment benefits and employee pensions.

Parliament approves Finland's accession to the European Union with a margin of 152 to 45.

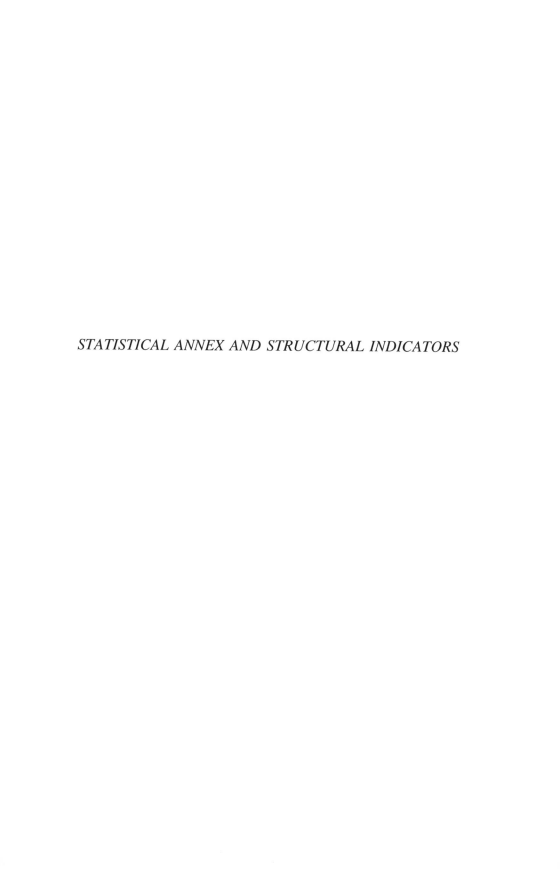

*STATISTICAL ANNEX AND STRUCTURAL INDICATORS*

Table A. **Selected background statistics**

| | Average 1984-93 | 1984 | 1985 | 1986 | 1987 | 1988 | 1989 | 1990 | 1991 | 1992 | 1993 |
|---|---|---|---|---|---|---|---|---|---|---|---|
| **A. Percentage changes** | | | | | | | | | | | |
| Private consumption[1] | 1.1 | 2.7 | 3.2 | 4.0 | 5.2 | 5.1 | 4.3 | 0 | -3.6 | -4.9 | -4.0 |
| Gross fixed capital formation[1] | -3.7 | -2.1 | 2.9 | -0.4 | 4.9 | 9.8 | 14.8 | -4.1 | -20.3 | -16.9 | -19.0 |
| Public investment[1] | 2.1 | 9.2 | 17.3 | -1.1 | 10.8 | 5.2 | -12.3 | 14.1 | -0.2 | -2.0 | -15.0 |
| Private investment[1] | -4.4 | -2.1 | 3.0 | -0.3 | 4.0 | 10.6 | 19.1 | -6.2 | -23.1 | -19.6 | -19.9 |
| GDP[1] | 1.0 | 3.1 | 3.3 | 2.4 | 4.1 | 4.9 | 5.7 | 0 | -7.1 | -3.6 | -2.0 |
| GDP price deflator | 4.8 | 8.8 | 5.4 | 4.6 | 4.7 | 7.0 | 6.1 | 5.8 | 2.5 | 0.8 | 2.5 |
| Industrial production | 1.9 | 4.8 | 4.3 | 1.7 | 4.4 | 4.1 | 2.6 | 0.4 | -9.6 | 2.4 | 5.1 |
| Employment | -1.6 | 1.0 | 1.0 | -0.3 | -0.3 | 0.3 | 1.6 | -0.1 | -5.2 | -7.1 | -6.1 |
| Compensation of employees (current prices) | 6.0 | 11.1 | 11.5 | 7.1 | 8.7 | 10.6 | 11.6 | 9.5 | 0.2 | -3.3 | -4.8 |
| Productivity (real GDP/employment) | 2.6 | 2.0 | 2.3 | 2.6 | 4.4 | 4.6 | 4.0 | 0.1 | -2.0 | 3.7 | 4.4 |
| Unit labour costs (compensation/real GDP) | 5.0 | 7.8 | 7.9 | 4.6 | 4.5 | 5.4 | 5.6 | 9.5 | 7.8 | 0.4 | -2.9 |
| **B. Percentage ratios** | | | | | | | | | | | |
| Gross fixed capital formation as per cent of GDP at constant prices | 24.1 | 25.3 | 25.2 | 24.6 | 24.8 | 25.9 | 28.1 | 27.0 | 23.2 | 20.0 | 16.5 |
| Stockbuilding as per cent of GDP at constant prices | -0.2 | 0.5 | -0.1 | -0.6 | -0.3 | 0.6 | 1.5 | 0.6 | -2.0 | -1.3 | -0.5 |
| Foreign balance as per cent of GDP at constant prices | 1.6 | 4.3 | 3.1 | 2.8 | 1.4 | -0.2 | -2.0 | -1.5 | -0.2 | 2.0 | 6.4 |
| Compensation of employees as per cent of GDP at current prices | 58.1 | 56.2 | 57.6 | 57.7 | 57.5 | 56.7 | 56.4 | 58.3 | 61.4 | 61.1 | 57.9 |
| Direct taxes as per cent of household income | 16.3 | 16.2 | 16.7 | 17.5 | 16.1 | 17.5 | 17.2 | 17.2 | 15.8 | 14.7 | 14.2 |
| Household saving as per cent of disposable income | 3.1 | 4.4 | 3.8 | 2.5 | 2.9 | -1.2 | -0.6 | 0.4 | 5.1 | 7.0 | 6.6 |
| Unemployment rate | 7.1 | 5.2 | 5.0 | 5.4 | 5.1 | 4.5 | 3.5 | 3.5 | 7.6 | 13.1 | 17.9 |
| **C. Other indicator** | | | | | | | | | | | |
| Current balance (billion dollars) | -3.1 | 0 | -0.8 | -0.7 | -1.7 | -2.7 | -5.8 | -6.9 | -6.7 | -4.9 | -1.0 |

1. At constant 1985 prices.

Table B. **Supply and use of ressources**

Mk million, current prices

| | 1984 | 1985 | 1986 | 1987 | 1988 | 1989 | 1990 | 1991 | 1992 | 1993 |
|---|---|---|---|---|---|---|---|---|---|---|
| Private consumption | 165 466 | 180 887 | 194 007 | 211 534 | 232 580 | 254 588 | 269 754 | 274 709 | 272 114 | 271 521 |
| | (9.1) | (10.2) | (6.9) | (9.8) | (11.7) | (13.5) | (6.3) | (-2.7) | (-5.0) | (-5.0) |
| Public consumption | 58 645 | 66 967 | 72 849 | 80 046 | 87 199 | 96 019 | 108 535 | 118 719 | 118 453 | 111 955 |
| Gross fixed investment | 72 849 | 79 423 | 82 908 | 92 541 | 109 258 | 136 148 | 139 144 | 110 061 | 87 953 | 71 272 |
| **Final domestic demand** | 296 961 | 327 277 | 349 764 | 384 121 | 429 037 | 486 755 | 517 433 | 503 489 | 478 520 | 454 748 |
| | (9.1) | (10.2) | (6.9) | (9.8) | (11.7) | (13.5) | (6.3) | (-2.7) | (-5.0) | (-5.0) |
| Stockbuilding | 1 511 | -440 | -2 211 | -889 | 3 006 | 6 424 | 2 924 | -9 498 | -5 833 | -2 876 |
| | (0.6) | (-0.6) | (-0.5) | (0.4) | (1.0) | (0.8) | (-0.7) | (-2.4) | (0.7) | (0.6) |
| **Total domestic demand** | 298 472 | 326 837 | 347 553 | 383 232 | 432 043 | 493 179 | 520 357 | 493 991 | 472 687 | 451 872 |
| | (9.7) | (9.5) | (6.3) | (10.3) | (12.7) | (14.2) | (5.5) | (-5.1) | (-4.3) | (-4.4) |
| Exports | 94 057 | 98 034 | 95 634 | 100 048 | 108 750 | 116 702 | 118 828 | 109 289 | 128 272 | 159 244 |
| Imports | 85 906 | 94 639 | 89 898 | 97 775 | 109 866 | 125 996 | 126 600 | 112 422 | 121 878 | 132 816 |
| **Foreign balance** | 8 053 | 3 395 | 5 736 | 2 273 | -1 116 | -9 294 | -7 772 | -3 133 | 6 394 | 26 428 |
| | (2.5) | (-1.5) | (0.7) | (-1.0) | (-0.9) | (-1.9) | (0.3) | (0.9) | (1.9) | (4.2) |
| Statistical discrepancy | -1 968 | 1 396 | 1 705 | 1 350 | 3 414 | 3 113 | 2 845 | 10 | -2 522 | 356 |
| **GDP (market prices)** | 305 266 | 331 628 | 354 994 | 386 855 | 434 341 | 486 998 | 515 430 | 490 868 | 476 559 | 478 656 |
| | (12.3) | (8.6) | (7.0) | (9.0) | (12.3) | (12.1) | (5.8) | (-4.8) | (-2.9) | (0.4) |

*Note:* Figures in parentheses are annual growth rates; for stockbuilding and the foreign balance they are contributions to GDP growth.
*Source:* Central Office of Statistics, *National Accounts.*

## Table C. Supply and use of resources
Mk million, 1990 prices

| | 1984 | 1985 | 1986 | 1987 | 1988 | 1989 | 1990 | 1991 | 1992 | 1993 |
|---|---|---|---|---|---|---|---|---|---|---|
| Private consumption | 218 034 | 225 002 | 234 000 | 246 163 | 258 821 | 269 879 | 269 754 | 260 031 | 247 363 | 237 559 |
| Public consumption | 88 343 | 92 900 | 95 792 | 99 878 | 102 132 | 104 526 | 108 535 | 111 256 | 108 799 | 102 932 |
| Gross fixed investment | 107 020 | 110 138 | 109 707 | 115 067 | 126 370 | 145 054 | 139 144 | 110 965 | 92 237 | 74 701 |
| **Final domestic demand** | 413 398 | 428 040 | 439 499 | 461 108 | 487 323 | 519 459 | 517 433 | 482 252 | 448 399 | 415 192 |
| | (1.5) | (3.5) | (2.7) | (4.9) | (5.7) | (6.6) | (−0.4) | (−6.8) | (−7.0) | (−7.4) |
| Stockbuilding | 1 993 | −577 | −2 620 | −1 321 | 2 967 | 7 978 | 2 924 | −9 567 | −6 071 | −2 358 |
| | (0.5) | (−0.6) | (−0.5) | (0.3) | (0.9) | (1.0) | (−1.0) | (−2.4) | (0.7) | (0.8) |
| **Total domestic demand** | 415 391 | 427 463 | 436 879 | 459 787 | 490 290 | 527 437 | 520 357 | 472 685 | 442 328 | 412 834 |
| | (2.0) | (2.9) | (2.2) | (5.2) | (6.6) | (7.6) | (−1.3) | (−9.2) | (−6.4) | (−6.7) |
| Exports | 106 075 | 107 365 | 108 673 | 111 632 | 115 761 | 117 241 | 118 828 | 110 965 | 122 059 | 142 292 |
| Imports | 87 897 | 93 868 | 96 281 | 105 175 | 116 898 | 127 311 | 126 600 | 111 755 | 112 989 | 113 352 |
| **Foreign balance** | 18 177 | 13 497 | 12 392 | 6 457 | −1 137 | −10 070 | −7 772 | −790 | 9 070 | 28 940 |
| | (1.1) | (−1.1) | (−0.3) | (−1.3) | (−1.6) | (−1.8) | (0.4) | (1.4) | (2.1) | (4.3) |
| Statistical discrepancy | −11 377 | −4 702 | −2 665 | −1 327 | −1 434 | −2 003 | 2 845 | 7 116 | 10 146 | 10 622 |
| **GDP (market prices)** | 422 192 | 436 258 | 446 606 | 464 917 | 487 719 | 515 364 | 515 430 | 479 011 | 461 544 | 452 396 |
| | (3.1) | (3.3) | (2.4) | (4.1) | (4.9) | (5.7) | (0) | (−7.1) | (−3.6) | (−2.0) |

*Note:* Figures in parentheses are annual growth rates; for stockbuilding and the foreign balance they are contributions to GDP growth.
*Source:* Central Statistical Office, *National Accounts.*

117

Table D. **Gross domestic product by industry of origin**

Mk million and percentage changes

| | 1983 | 1984 | 1985 | 1986 | 1987 | 1988 | 1989 | 1990 | 1991 | 1992 |
|---|---|---|---|---|---|---|---|---|---|---|
| **At current prices** (Mk million) | | | | | | | | | | |
| Agriculture, forestry and fishing | 21 369 | 23 580 | 24 310 | 24 239 | 22 612 | 24 739 | 28 077 | 29 043 | 24 073 | 21 061 |
| Industry[1] | 72 407 | 80 146 | 85 331 | 88 946 | 98 409 | 107 640 | 116 507 | 116 620 | 102 455 | 105 375 |
| Manufacturing | 63 496 | 70 911 | 75 644 | 78 197 | 87 145 | 95 972 | 105 225 | 105 383 | 89 667 | 92 811 |
| Electricity, gas and water | 7 826 | 8 050 | 8 429 | 9 522 | 10 018 | 10 065 | 9 245 | 9 504 | 11 059 | 10 886 |
| Construction | 20 887 | 22 750 | 23 222 | 25 199 | 27 461 | 32 940 | 42 035 | 43 467 | 36 962 | 25 944 |
| Services | 134 410 | 151 191 | 168 578 | 183 866 | 202 210 | 224 058 | 250 860 | 275 982 | 279 615 | 272 645 |
| Market services | 94 923 | 106 646 | 118 130 | 129 044 | 141 977 | 157 967 | 177 645 | 193 834 | 188 832 | 182 028 |
| Public administration | 39 487 | 44 545 | 50 448 | 54 822 | 60 233 | 66 091 | 73 215 | 82 148 | 90 783 | 90 617 |
| GDP (at factor costs) | 249 073 | 277 667 | 301 441 | 322 250 | 350 692 | 389 377 | 437 479 | 465 112 | 443 105 | 425 025 |
| **At 1990 prices** (Percentage changes) | | | | | | | | | | |
| Agriculture, forestry and fishing | 3.1 | 2.3 | -0.7 | -5.4 | -8.0 | 5.5 | 7.5 | 2.5 | -11.1 | -3.3 |
| Industry[1] | 2.7 | 4.5 | 4.2 | 2.0 | 6.0 | 4.0 | 3.8 | -0.4 | -9.7 | 2.3 |
| Manufacturing | 2.6 | 4.4 | 3.8 | 2.0 | 5.9 | 4.1 | 4.0 | -0.7 | -10.9 | 2.7 |
| Electricity, gas and water | 4.4 | 6.3 | 8.5 | 0.6 | 7.2 | 2.7 | 0 | 1.9 | 3.1 | -0.9 |
| Construction | 4.3 | -2.7 | 0.9 | 2.0 | 1.3 | 9.2 | 14.1 | -2.3 | -11.6 | -15.2 |
| Services | 3.4 | 3.7 | 3.9 | 3.6 | 4.9 | 4.2 | 5.4 | 1.5 | -4.0 | -4.8 |
| Market services | 3.5 | 4.5 | 4.5 | 4.5 | 5.6 | 4.9 | 6.9 | 1.5 | -6.3 | -6.0 |
| Public administration | 3.1 | 2.2 | 2.8 | 1.6 | 3.5 | 2.6 | 2.0 | 1.5 | 1.2 | -2.2 |
| GDP (at factor costs) | 3.3 | 3.2 | 3.4 | 2.4 | 4.0 | 4.7 | 5.9 | 0.7 | -6.6 | -3.9 |

1. Including mining.

Source: OECD, National Accounts.

118

Table E. **General government account**

Mk million

| | 1984 | 1985 | 1986 | 1987 | 1988 | 1989 | 1990 | 1991 | 1992 | 1993 |
|---|---|---|---|---|---|---|---|---|---|---|
| Current receipts | 137 188 | 155 263 | 170 929 | 178 408 | 208 936 | 235 265 | 261 587 | 257 530 | 253 866 | 257 159 |
| Direct taxes | 49 381 | 55 741 | 63 127 | 61 308 | 74 454 | 82 179 | 92 741 | 88 138 | 82 270 | 74 900 |
| Social security contributions | 32 457 | 38 543 | 41 312 | 44 800 | 50 329 | 56 673 | 67 243 | 68 137 | 70 882 | 79 154 |
| Indirect taxes | 43 380 | 47 639 | 52 316 | 57 388 | 66 667 | 75 595 | 78 025 | 74 730 | 71 643 | 71 556 |
| Other current receipts | 11 970 | 13 340 | 14 174 | 14 912 | 17 486 | 20 818 | 23 578 | 26 525 | 29 071 | 31 549 |
| Current expenditure | 120 457 | 136 974 | 149 699 | 163 777 | 176 535 | 194 731 | 221 029 | 251 973 | 271 327 | 284 122 |
| Expenditure on goods and services | 58 842 | 66 967 | 72 849 | 80 046 | 87 199 | 96 019 | 108 535 | 118 719 | 118 453 | 111 955 |
| Subsidies | 9 791 | 10 347 | 11 308 | 11 684 | 11 271 | 13 717 | 14 756 | 17 174 | 17 028 | 16 319 |
| Interest paid | 5 218 | 6 147 | 6 195 | 6 571 | 7 201 | 7 260 | 7 511 | 9 598 | 12 608 | 22 401 |
| Social benefits | 42 544 | 48 955 | 54 164 | 59 465 | 64 044 | 69 930 | 81 195 | 96 396 | 112 924 | 122 615 |
| Other current transfers | 4 062 | 4 558 | 5 183 | 6 011 | 6 820 | 7 805 | 9 032 | 10 086 | 10 314 | 10 832 |
| Saving | 16 730 | 18 289 | 21 230 | 14 631 | 32 401 | 40 534 | 40 558 | 5 557 | -17 461 | -26 963 |
| Fixed investment | 9 862 | 10 877 | 11 281 | 13 371 | 15 046 | 14 295 | 17 286 | 17 067 | 15 897 | 13 227 |
| Capital transfers, net | -96 | -94 | -539 | -588 | -3 277 | -870 | -757 | -1 202 | -896 | -684 |
| Consumption of fixed capital | 3 622 | 4 014 | 4 470 | 5 067 | 5 696 | 6 294 | 7 383 | 7 481 | 7 401 | 7 538 |
| Net lending | 9 166 | 9 882 | 12 291 | 4 275 | 17 986 | 30 720 | 27 800 | -7 209 | -27 869 | -34 091 |
| (as a percentage of GDP) | 3.0 | 3.0 | 3.5 | 1.1 | 4.1 | 6.3 | 5.4 | -1.5 | -5.8 | -7.1 |

*Source:* OECD, *National Accounts.*

119

Table F. **Balance of payments**

Million US dollars

| | 1984 | 1985 | 1986 | 1987 | 1988 | 1989 | 1990 | 1991 | 1992 | 1993 |
|---|---|---|---|---|---|---|---|---|---|---|
| *Current account* | | | | | | | | | | |
| Merchandise exports | 13 099 | 13 286 | 15 962 | 19 038 | 21 786 | 22 877 | 26 060 | 22 492 | 23 545 | 23 098 |
| **Trade balance** | 1 489 | 911 | 1 622 | 1 382 | 1 111 | -221 | 724 | 2 362 | 3 948 | 6 383 |
| Services, net | -1 344 | -1 509 | -1 947 | -2 609 | -3 311 | -4 816 | -6 686 | -7 976 | -8 055 | -6 798 |
| Travel | -192 | -277 | -459 | -683 | -852 | -1 023 | -1 588 | -1 483 | -1 075 | -368 |
| Investment income | -1 140 | -1 060 | -1 382 | -1 636 | -1 829 | -2 721 | -3 724 | -4 618 | -5 350 | -4 984 |
| Other services | -12 | -172 | -106 | -290 | -630 | -1 072 | -1 374 | -1 875 | -1 630 | -1 446 |
| Transfers, net | -175 | -177 | -391 | -490 | -508 | -764 | -973 | -1 062 | -807 | -551 |
| Private | -22 | -6 | -157 | -161 | -87 | -253 | -337 | -306 | -279 | -99 |
| **Current balance** | -30 | -774 | -716 | -1 718 | -2 707 | -5 800 | -6 936 | -6 677 | -4 914 | -966 |
| *Capital account* | | | | | | | | | | |
| Long-term capital, net | 656 | 913 | -283 | 15 | 716 | 1 475 | 7 772 | 11 607 | 8 579 | 6 995 |
| Private, direct | -355 | -242 | -470 | -876 | -2 078 | -2 619 | -2 476 | -1 296 | -10 | -1 238 |
| Private, portfolio | 1 277 | 1 342 | 1 346 | 1 408 | 3 131 | 3 399 | 5 776 | 9 314 | 8 116 | 5 748 |
| Public[1] | 97 | -45 | -109 | -144 | -543 | -442 | -220 | 214 | 268 | 805 |
| Short-term capital, net | 1 990 | 869 | -1 304 | 6 566 | 1 131 | 1 623 | 4 766 | -6 324 | -5 410 | -6 358 |
| Private non monetary | 1 078 | -464 | -770 | 786 | -928 | 964 | -86 | -1 453 | 933 | 332 |
| Private monetary institutions | 912 | 1 333 | -534 | 5 780 | 2 059 | 659 | 4 852 | -4 871 | -6 343 | -6 690 |
| Miscellaneous official accounts | 193 | -9 | -743 | 28 | 93 | 491 | 256 | -239 | 468 | -328 |
| Allocation of SDRs | 0 | 0 | 0 | 0 | 0 | 0 | 0 | 0 | 0 | 0 |
| Errors and omissions | -521 | -109 | 443 | -1 572 | 817 | 1 289 | -2 454 | -389 | -1 119 | 955 |
| Change in reserves | 1 775 | 613 | -2 307 | 4 063 | 137 | -1 057 | 4 033 | -1 825 | -2 046 | 213 |

1. Excludes special transactions.
*Source:* OECD Secretariat.

Table G. **Labour market**

| | 1984 | 1985 | 1986 | 1987 | 1988 | 1989 | 1990 | 1991 | 1992 | 1993 |
|---|---|---|---|---|---|---|---|---|---|---|
| **Labour force surveys** | | | | | | | | | | |
| Labour force (thousands) | 2 546 | 2 566 | 2 569 | 2 554 | 2 546 | 2 559 | 2 556 | 2 533 | 2 502 | 2 484 |
| Employment (thousands) | 2 414 | 2 437 | 2 431 | 2 423 | 2 431 | 2 470 | 2 467 | 2 340 | 2 174 | 2 041 |
| Unemployment rate (per cent) | 5.2 | 5.0 | 5.4 | 5.1 | 4.5 | 5.5 | 3.5 | 7.6 | 13.1 | 17.9 |
| **Employment exchange services** | | | | | | | | | | |
| Unemployed persons seeking work | | | | | | | | | | |
| Total (thousands) | 135.3 | 141.5 | 150.7 | 142.5 | 129.3 | 104.5 | 105.4 | 213.2 | 363.1 | 482.2 |
| Insured (thousands) | 60.1 | 64.0 | 70.8 | 64.3 | 58.4 | 47.9 | 48.9 | 109.5 | 194.4 | 268.2 |
| Unfilled vacancies (thousands) | 12.0 | 12.2 | 12.4 | 12.4 | 17.4 | 30.4 | 26.9 | 13.4 | 7.1 | 5.9 |

*Source:* Ministry of Labour, *Finnish Labour Rewiew.*

Table H. **Imports: prices, volumes and values by commodity group**

|  | 1984 | 1985 | 1986 | 1987 | 1988 | 1989 | 1990 | 1991 | 1992 | 1993 |
|---|---|---|---|---|---|---|---|---|---|---|
| **Import unit values** (1980 = 100) | | | | | | | | | | |
| Total | 131 | 135 | 121 | 119 | 122 | 126 | 128 | 131 | 145 | 163 |
| Raw materials | 131 | 134 | 115 | 112 | 116 | 121 | 120 | 123 | 136 | 155 |
| Fuels and lubricants | 132 | 129 | 78 | 68 | 60 | 68 | 72 | 73 | 75 | 82 |
| Investment goods | 128 | 134 | 140 | 141 | 147 | 146 | 153 | 157 | 181 | 211 |
| Consumer goods | 132 | 142 | 149 | 146 | 151 | 155 | 161 | 166 | 177 | 191 |
| **Volume of imports** (1980 = 100) | | | | | | | | | | |
| Total | 98 | 104 | 110 | 119 | 130 | 144 | 138 | 115 | 112 | 109 |
| Raw materials | 93 | 99 | 102 | 109 | 112 | 122 | 119 | 103 | 105 | 102 |
| Fuels and lubricants | 93 | 104 | 124 | 123 | 125 | 117 | 121 | 106 | 122 | 139 |
| Investment goods | 107 | 109 | 115 | 125 | 147 | 176 | 158 | 111 | 92 | 91 |
| Consumer goods | 116 | 123 | 136 | 158 | 186 | 208 | 200 | 172 | 159 | 148 |
| **Value of imports (cif)** (Mk million) | | | | | | | | | | |
| Total | 74 682 | 81 520 | 77 601 | 82 807 | 92 118 | 105 519 | 103 027 | 87 744 | 94 947 | 103 078 |
| Raw materials | 47 028 | 50 944 | 45 413 | 47 130 | 50 267 | 56 845 | 55 473 | 48 787 | 55 471 | 61 031 |
| Fuels and lubricants | 5 034 | 5 502 | 3 949 | 3 450 | 3 056 | 3 252 | 3 571 | 3 137 | 3 740 | 4 658 |
| Investment goods | 10 993 | 11 675 | 12 898 | 14 138 | 17 274 | 20 605 | 19 365 | 13 972 | 13 352 | 15 337 |
| Consumer goods | 11 454 | 12 967 | 15 069 | 17 478 | 20 828 | 24 056 | 23 889 | 21 193 | 20 826 | 21 045 |

*Source*: Central Statistical Office, *Bulletin of Statistics*.

Table I. Exports: prices, volumes and values by commodity group

| | 1984 | 1985 | 1986 | 1987 | 1988 | 1989 | 1990 | 1991 | 1992 | 1993 |
|---|---|---|---|---|---|---|---|---|---|---|
| **Export unit values** (1980 = 100) | | | | | | | | | | |
| Total | 134 | 138 | 135 | 138 | 145 | 156 | 154 | 154 | 164 | 172 |
| Wood | 124 | 118 | 119 | 123 | 130 | 140 | 157 | 155 | 164 | 164 |
| Paper | 134 | 137 | 132 | 134 | 143 | 150 | 144 | 139 | 144 | 151 |
| Metal and engines | 145 | 150 | 162 | 170 | 176 | 191 | 199 | 206 | 222 | 229 |
| **Volume of exports** (1980 = 100) | | | | | | | | | | |
| Total | 114 | 115 | 116 | 118 | 121 | 121 | 125 | 114 | 124 | 147 |
| Wood | 74 | 74 | 75 | 78 | 75 | 68 | 64 | 58 | 62 | 86 |
| Paper | 112 | 116 | 118 | 128 | 135 | 138 | 139 | 136 | 143 | 157 |
| Metal and engines | 138 | 141 | 140 | 134 | 144 | 148 | 154 | 123 | 139 | 181 |
| **Value of exports (fob)** (Mk million) | | | | | | | | | | |
| Total | 80 904 | 84 028 | 82 579 | 85 516 | 92 902 | 99 782 | 101 327 | 92 886 | 107 463 | 133 927 |
| Agriculture | 2 550 | 2 381 | 2 209 | 2 195 | 1 421 | 1 406 | 885 | 1 053 | 1 088 | 1 729 |
| Manufacturing | 77 996 | 81 208 | 80 028 | 82 993 | 91 099 | 97 862 | 99 994 | 91 300 | 105 876 | 131 642 |
| Wood | 7 145 | 6 728 | 6 947 | 7 470 | 7 567 | 7 417 | 7 810 | 6 986 | 7 892 | 10 889 |
| Paper | 23 573 | 25 030 | 24 600 | 27 058 | 30 474 | 32 513 | 31 668 | 29 693 | 32 587 | 37 410 |
| Metal and engines | 22 998 | 24 412 | 26 115 | 26 230 | 29 225 | 32 682 | 35 492 | 29 189 | 35 740 | 48 099 |

*Sources:* Central Statistical Office, *Bulletin of Statistics*.

Table J. **Foreign trade by area**
Million US dollars

| | 1984 | 1985 | 1986 | 1987 | 1988 | 1989 | 1990 | 1991 | 1992 | 1993 |
|---|---|---|---|---|---|---|---|---|---|---|
| **Imports, total** | 12 435 | 13 226 | 15 326 | 19 860 | 20 911 | 24 611 | 27 098 | 21 708 | 20 741 | 18 026 |
| OECD countries | 8 220 | 8 943 | 11 366 | 15 050 | 16 102 | 19 203 | 21 574 | 17 147 | 16 129 | 14 081 |
| EEC | 4 616 | 5 106 | 6 575 | 8 786 | 9 038 | 10 890 | 12 405 | 9 886 | 9 595 | 8 219 |
| *of which:* Germany | 1 730 | 1 973 | 2 591 | 3 454 | 3 514 | 4 248 | 4 603 | 3 666 | 3 449 | 2 938 |
| Belgium-Luxembourg | 241 | 265 | 373 | 509 | 525 | 677 | 741 | 557 | 587 | 528 |
| France | 393 | 446 | 682 | 835 | 829 | 1 004 | 1 151 | 867 | 853 | 707 |
| Netherlands | 340 | 389 | 464 | 612 | 665 | 788 | 859 | 729 | 735 | 647 |
| United Kingdom | 957 | 947 | 993 | 1 415 | 1 401 | 1 605 | 2 053 | 1 653 | 1 791 | 1 589 |
| USA | 624 | 715 | 731 | 1 042 | 1 326 | 1 553 | 1 833 | 1 481 | 1 263 | 1 313 |
| Sweden | 1 530 | 1 554 | 2 049 | 2 545 | 2 786 | 3 338 | 3 506 | 2 606 | 2 353 | 1 837 |
| Norway | 259 | 317 | 329 | 416 | 470 | 541 | 893 | 963 | 818 | 860 |
| Non OECD countries | 4 215 | 4 210 | 3 861 | 4 636 | 4 604 | 5 196 | 5 320 | 4 374 | 4 239 | 3 741 |
| COMECON | 3 259 | 3 126 | 2 779 | 3 287 | 2 943 | 3 368 | 3 238 | 2 334 | 2 062 | 2 010 |
| OPEC | 172 | 232 | 159 | 180 | 116 | 128 | 164 | 269 | 270 | 69 |
| Others | 784 | 851 | 924 | 1 170 | 1 545 | 1 699 | 1 918 | 1 770 | 1 907 | 1 661 |
| **Exports, total** | 13 498 | 13 609 | 16 326 | 20 039 | 21 639 | 23 265 | 26 718 | 23 081 | 23 515 | 23 491 |
| OECD countries | 9 259 | 8 999 | 11 278 | 14 668 | 15 886 | 17 226 | 19 961 | 18 351 | 18 822 | 17 390 |
| EEC | 5 164 | 4 943 | 6 164 | 8 327 | 9 321 | 9 951 | 12 060 | 11 456 | 12 121 | 10 660 |
| *of which:* Germany | 1 265 | 1 225 | 1 552 | 2 157 | 2 263 | 2 433 | 3 204 | 3 445 | 3 566 | 2 981 |
| Belgium-Luxembourg | 190 | 196 | 268 | 347 | 404 | 425 | 549 | 558 | 571 | 483 |
| France | 526 | 527 | 722 | 1 049 | 1 125 | 1 238 | 1 601 | 1 322 | 1 531 | 1 205 |
| Netherlands | 464 | 443 | 558 | 703 | 775 | 903 | 1 117 | 1 118 | 1 187 | 1 148 |
| United Kingdom | 1 610 | 1 448 | 1 690 | 2 253 | 2 776 | 2 732 | 2 766 | 2 329 | 2 451 | 2 393 |
| USA | 1 093 | 847 | 875 | 1 026 | 1 236 | 1 480 | 1 545 | 1 402 | 1 383 | 1 809 |
| Sweden | 1 653 | 1 781 | 2 400 | 2 974 | 3 021 | 3 294 | 3 749 | 3 138 | 2 957 | 2 548 |
| Norway | 611 | 569 | 732 | 943 | 739 | 675 | 799 | 751 | 812 | 734 |
| Non OECD countries | 4 086 | 4 439 | 4 840 | 5 108 | 5 292 | 5 539 | 6 128 | 4 130 | 4 088 | 5 462 |
| COMECON | 2 773 | 3 164 | 3 554 | 3 383 | 3 500 | 3 721 | 3 728 | 1 531 | 1 547 | 2 186 |
| OPEC | 319 | 304 | 232 | 261 | 265 | 261 | 275 | 277 | 245 | 264 |
| Others | 994 | 971 | 1 053 | 1 464 | 1 527 | 1 557 | 2 125 | 2 323 | 2 297 | 3 012 |

*Source:* OECD, *Foreign Trade Statistics, Series B.*

Table K.  **Prices and wages**

|  | 1984 | 1985 | 1986 | 1987 | 1988 | 1989 | 1990 | 1991 | 1992 | 1993 |
|---|---|---|---|---|---|---|---|---|---|---|
| **Consumer prices**<br>(1990 = 100) | | | | | | | | | | |
| Total | 75 | 79 | 81 | 84 | 89 | 94 | 100 | 104 | 107 | 110 |
| Food | 80 | 86 | 90 | 91 | 93 | 97 | 100 | 103 | 103 | 102 |
| Rent and energy | 69 | 73 | 73 | 74 | 80 | 93 | 100 | 102 | 102 | 97 |
| **Wholesale prices**<br>(1990 = 100) | | | | | | | | | | |
| Total | 86 | 90 | 87 | 89 | 92 | 96 | 100 | 100 | 103 | 108 |
| Domestic goods | 83 | 87 | 85 | 87 | 91 | 96 | 100 | 100 | 101 | 104 |
| Imported goods | 94 | 98 | 93 | 93 | 95 | 99 | 100 | 101 | 107 | 117 |
| Building costs | 71 | 75 | 78 | 81 | 87 | 93 | 100 | 102 | 100 | 101 |
| **Wage and salary earnings**<br>(1990 = 100) | | | | | | | | | | |
| Total | 62 | 68 | 72 | 77 | 84 | 92 | 100 | 106 | 109 | 106 |
| Industry | 63 | 68 | 72 | 77 | 84 | 89 | 100 | 106 | 108 | 110 |
| Workers | 62 | 67 | 71 | 76 | 83 | 91 | 100 | 106 | 107 | 107 |
| Private | 62 | 67 | 72 | 77 | 84 | 92 | 100 | 106 | 108 | 109 |
| Local Government | 64 | 69 | 74 | 79 | 84 | 91 | 100 | 107 | 110 | 112 |
| Central Government | 62 | 67 | 71 | 77 | 86 | 92 | 100 | 105 | 107 | 108 |

*Source:* Central Statistical Office, *Bulletin of Statistics.*

125

Table L. **Interest rates, money and credit**

| | 1984 | 1985 | 1986 | 1987 | 1988 | 1989 | 1990 | 1991 | 1992 | 1993 |
|---|---|---|---|---|---|---|---|---|---|---|
| **Interest rates** | | | | | | | | | | |
| Bank of Finland base rate[1] | 9.5 | 9.0 | 7.5 | 7.0 | 7.6 | 7.7 | 8.5 | 8.5 | 9.2 | 6.9 |
| Call money rate[1] | 16.5 | 13.4 | 13.4 | 11.7 | 11.5 | 13.4 | 15.0 | 15.5 | 14.9 | 14.9 |
| Average lending rate of commercial banks[2] | 10.7 | 10.4 | 8.8 | 9.0 | 9.9 | 10.6 | 11.8 | 12.1 | 12.5 | 10.2 |
| **Bank of Finland net claims on:** | | | | | | | | | | |
| Foreign sector | 17 576 | 21 225 | 13 218 | 29 734 | 30 263 | 22 752 | 35 959 | 33 204 | 26 519 | 32 148 |
| Public sector | -2 326 | -3 277 | -999 | 76 | -775 | -4 188 | -7 | 1 372 | 2 356 | 1 004 |
| Financial institutions | -2 713 | -2 897 | 4 343 | -6 618 | -4 864 | 12 751 | -2 664 | 4 846 | -5 405 | 476 |
| Corporate sector | 2 032 | 412 | -176 | -1 333 | -3 756 | -8 604 | -8 247 | -5 768 | -1 904 | 1 216 |
| Banks' credit to the public[3] | 124 157 | 146 451 | 166 231 | 192 382 | 251 546 | 278 688 | 285 720 | 285 609 | 271 544 | 264 846 |
| **Money** | | | | | | | | | | |
| Money supply M1 | 84 390 | 93 215 | 96 874 | 105 829 | 111 259 | 124 295 | 141 524 | 129 769 | 134 829 | 141 759 |
| M1 plus quasi money | 132 965 | 155 212 | 169 095 | 190 837 | 234 268 | 251 519 | 266 383 | 274 365 | 274 011 | 279 595 |

1. Average of daily observations.
2. End of period.
3. Credits in million Markka.
Source: Bank of Finland, Monthly Bulletin.

# Table M. Production structure and performance indicators

### A. Production structure

| | Share of value added (per cent)[1] | | | | | | Share of employment (per cent) | | | | | |
|---|---|---|---|---|---|---|---|---|---|---|---|---|
| | 1960 | 1970 | 1980 | 1985 | 1991 | 1992 | 1960 | 1970 | 1980 | 1985 | 1991 | 1992 |
| **Tradeables** | | | | | | | | | | | | |
| Manufacturing | 27.9 | 30.5 | 32.9 | 30.8 | 26.1 | 28.6 | 22.5 | 27.7 | 31.3 | 29.3 | 26.8 | 26.8 |
| *of which:* | | | | | | | | | | | | |
| Food, beverages and tobacco | 4.2 | 4.0 | 3.5 | 3.6 | 3.8 | 4.0 | 2.6 | 3.4 | 3.6 | 3.4 | 3.3 | 3.4 |
| Textile, wearing apparels and leather industries | 3.4 | 3.0 | 2.8 | 2.1 | 1.0 | 1.0 | 4.5 | 4.5 | 4.1 | 3.3 | 1.8 | 1.7 |
| Wood and wood products, including furniture | 3.2 | 2.8 | 2.9 | 1.5 | 1.3 | 1.6 | 3.2 | 3.5 | 3.0 | 2.3 | 1.9 | 1.9 |
| Paper and paper products, printing and publishing | 5.3 | 6.6 | 7.2 | 6.8 | 5.4 | 6.1 | 3.4 | 4.3 | 5.2 | 5.0 | 5.0 | 5.1 |
| Chemical and chemical products, petroleum, coal, rubber and plastic products | 2.0 | 3.1 | 3.9 | 3.4 | 3.2 | 3.2 | 1.0 | 1.9 | 2.3 | 2.2 | 2.3 | 2.4 |
| Non-metallic mineral products, except products of petroleum and coal | 1.1 | 1.3 | 1.3 | 1.3 | 1.2 | 1.1 | 0.9 | 1.2 | 1.2 | 1.2 | 1.2 | 1.1 |
| Basic metal industries | 0.7 | 1.3 | 1.6 | 1.3 | 1.2 | 1.6 | 0.5 | 0.8 | 1.1 | 1.1 | 1.0 | 1.0 |
| Fabricated metal products, machinery and equipment | 7.5 | 8.0 | 8.5 | 9.8 | 8.2 | 9.0 | 5.9 | 7.8 | 9.5 | 9.6 | 9.1 | 9.0 |
| Other manufacturing industries | 0.4 | 0.3 | 1.2 | 1.0 | 0.9 | 0.9 | 0.4 | 0.3 | 1.4 | 1.3 | 1.2 | 1.1 |
| **Non-tradeables** | | | | | | | | | | | | |
| Agriculture and forestry | 20.5 | 14.2 | 11.4 | 9.9 | 7.0 | 6.5 | 39.2 | 25.0 | 16.6 | 15.2 | 12.0 | 12.5 |
| Mining and quarrying | 0.7 | 1.0 | 0.6 | 0.5 | 0.5 | 0.5 | 0.3 | 0.3 | 0.5 | 0.4 | 0.3 | 0.3 |
| Electricity, gas and water | 3.4 | 3.1 | 3.4 | 3.4 | 3.2 | 3.3 | 0.9 | 1.1 | 1.6 | 1.6 | 1.6 | 1.7 |
| Construction | 11.0 | 11.2 | 9.3 | 9.5 | 10.8 | 8.0 | 11.0 | 11.2 | 9.8 | 10.2 | 11.1 | 10.1 |
| Wholesale and retail trade, restaurants and hotels | 12.1 | 12.6 | 15.1 | 16.0 | 15.2 | 15.6 | 13.3 | 17.7 | 19.7 | 20.7 | 22.1 | 21.9 |
| Transport, storage and communication | 8.7 | 9.1 | 9.2 | 9.6 | 10.5 | 11.1 | 6.8 | 7.8 | 9.0 | 9.2 | 10.0 | 10.4 |
| Finance, insurance, real estate and business services | 12.5 | 14.3 | 15.7 | 17.7 | 23.0 | 22.6 | 2.8 | 4.3 | 7.2 | 8.9 | 11.9 | 11.9 |
| Community, social and personal services | 3.2 | 4.0 | 2.4 | 2.7 | 3.6 | 3.8 | 3.2 | 4.8 | 4.4 | 4.4 | 4.3 | 4.5 |

| | Share of total GDP (per cent) | | | | | | Share of total employment (per cent) | | | | | |
|---|---|---|---|---|---|---|---|---|---|---|---|---|
| **As a share of total GDP** | 100.0 | 100.0 | 100.0 | 100.0 | 100.0 | 100.0 | 100.0 | 100.0 | 100.0 | 100.0 | 100.0 | 100.0 |
| Private GDP | 88.3 | 85.5 | 83.8 | 81.4 | 77.4 | 76.5 | 85.8 | 82.2 | 79.6 | 77.3 | 73.8 | 72.5 |
| Public sector | 9.3 | 12.1 | 14.5 | 16.7 | 20.5 | 21.3 | 7.7 | 11.7 | 17.9 | 20.1 | 23.3 | 24.5 |
| Other producers | 2.4 | 2.4 | 1.7 | 1.9 | 2.1 | 2.2 | 6.5 | 6.2 | 2.6 | 2.6 | 2.9 | 3.0 |

1. At factor costs.

Table M. **Production structure and performance indicators** *(cont'd)*

B. Sector performance

| | Productivity growth (Sector GDP/sector employment) | | | | | Investment Per cent of total industry investment[1] | | | | | |
|---|---|---|---|---|---|---|---|---|---|---|---|
| | 1960-69 | 1970-79 | 1980-87 | 1991 | 1992 | 1960 | 1970 | 1980 | 1985 | 1991 | 1992 |
| **Tradeables** | | | | | | | | | | | |
| Manufacturing | 4.6 | 2.7 | 5.1 | -3.8 | 12.5 | 20.0 | 24.0 | 21.0 | 19.6 | 17.4 | 20.2 |
| *of which:* | | | | | | | | | | | |
| Food, beverages and tobacco | 3.1 | 1.6 | 3.1 | 1.5 | 9.4 | — | — | 2.7 | 2.0 | 2.2 | 3.9 |
| Textile, wearing apparels and leather industries | 4.9 | 4.0 | 4.0 | 0.7 | 7.1 | — | — | 1.0 | 0.4 | 0.2 | 0.2 |
| Wood and wood products, including furniture | 3.3 | 5.9 | 5.8 | -11.2 | 15.8 | — | — | 1.8 | 0.9 | 1.1 | 1.1 |
| Paper and paper products, printing and publishing | 4.0 | 1.4 | 4.9 | -1.0 | 8.0 | — | — | 6.0 | 6.8 | 6.9 | 7.4 |
| Chemical and chemical products, petroleum, coal, rubber and plastic products | 8.1 | 2.8 | 3.5 | -3.3 | 7.1 | — | — | 2.5 | 2.4 | 2.2 | 2.9 |
| Non-metallic mineral products, except products of petroleum and coal | 7.6 | 3.0 | 4.1 | -7.0 | 9.1 | — | — | 0.9 | 0.8 | 0.5 | 0.5 |
| Basic metal industries | 7.1 | 2.9 | 5.3 | 3.4 | 18.5 | — | — | 1.3 | 1.1 | 1.1 | 0.9 |
| Fabricated metal products, machinery and equipment | 2.9 | 3.8 | 5.9 | -9.8 | 18.1 | — | — | 4.3 | 4.7 | 3.0 | 3.0 |
| Other manufacturing industries | 11.9 | -14.0 | 4.1 | -3.0 | 10.3 | — | — | 0.4 | 0.5 | 0.3 | 0.3 |
| **Non-tradeables** | | | | | | | | | | | |
| Agriculture and forestry | 5.4 | 4.9 | 0.5 | -7.1 | 2.3 | 11.5 | 8.8 | 11.0 | 9.4 | 6.1 | 5.6 |
| Mining and quarrying | 4.9 | 0.1 | 11.5 | -7.8 | -2.3 | 0.6 | 0.5 | 0.5 | 0.5 | 0.2 | 0.2 |
| Electricity, gas and water | 5.1 | 2.0 | 3.7 | 6.9 | 3.0 | 8.9 | 5.5 | 5.4 | 6.2 | 6.5 | 6.9 |
| Construction | 2.9 | 3.2 | 0.4 | 1.1 | 1.5 | 2.9 | 2.9 | 2.4 | 1.5 | 2.0 | 0.9 |
| Wholesale and retail trade, restaurants and hotels | 2.4 | 2.6 | 2.7 | -5.4 | 0.8 | 10.1 | 8.9 | 7.4 | 9.3 | 10.4 | 10.6 |
| Transport, storage and communication | 3.5 | 2.3 | 2.0 | 3.9 | 5.0 | 15.1 | 11.8 | 11.4 | 8.8 | 7.6 | 10.6 |
| Finance, insurance, real estate and business services | 0.8 | 0 | 0.5 | 1.0 | 1.1 | 28.3 | 35.1 | 38.7 | 42.3 | 46.3 | 41.6 |
| *of which:* | | | | | | | | | | | |
| Dwellings | — | — | — | — | — | — | — | 34.2 | 31.6 | 33.9 | 32.7 |
| Community, social and personal services | 1.7 | 2.6 | 2.8 | 0.9 | -0.5 | 2.5 | 2.5 | 2.3 | 2.4 | 3.5 | 3.5 |
| | | | | | | Per cent of total investment | | | | | |
| Private sector | 4.7 | 3.4 | 3.2 | -1.4 | 4.7 | 84.1 | 86.5 | 85.4 | 85.2 | 82.9 | 80.8 |
| Public sector | 0 | 0.5 | 0.2 | 0.2 | 0.3 | 14.7 | 12.4 | 13.3 | 13.7 | 15.5 | 17.5 |
| Other producers | 1.5 | 9.6 | 1.4 | -1.2 | -0.3 | 1.2 | 1.2 | 1.4 | 1.2 | 1.6 | 1.7 |

1. Current prices.

|  | 1983 | 1989 | 1990 | 1991 | 1992 | 1993 |
|---|---|---|---|---|---|---|
| **Budget indicators: General government**<br>**(per cent of GDP)** | | | | | | |
| Current receipts | 43.0 | 48.3 | 50.8 | 52.5 | 53.3 | 53.7 |
| Non-interest expenditure | 37.9 | 38.5 | 41.4 | 49.4 | 54.3 | 54.7 |
| Primary budget balance | −1.1 | 4.5 | 3.0 | −4.2 | −8.5 | −8.3 |
| Net interest expenses | −1.7 | −1.9 | −2.4 | −2.7 | −2.7 | −1.1 |
| General government budget balance | 0.6 | 6.3 | 5.4 | −1.5 | −5.9 | −7.1 |
| **Structure of expenditure and taxation**<br>**(per cent of GDP)** | | | | | | |
| Expenditure | 43.6 | 43.1 | 46.7 | 55.2 | 60.5 | 62.3 |
| Income transfers (including interest payments) | 15.6 | 15.9 | 17.2 | 21.6 | 26.4 | 30.3 |
| Capital transfers | 1.3 | 1.6 | 1.7 | 2.1 | 2.2 | 2.3 |
| Subsidies | 3.3 | 2.8 | 2.9 | 3.5 | 3.6 | 3.4 |
| Consumption | 19.3 | 19.7 | 21.1 | 24.2 | 24.9 | 23.4 |
| Education | 5.1 | 5.1 | 5.3 | 6.1 | 6.2 | 5.7 |
| Health | 4.2 | 4.4 | 4.8 | 5.4 | 5.5 | 5.2 |
| Social welfare | 3.1 | 3.8 | 4.2 | 4.8 | 4.8 | 4.5 |
| Housing | 0.7 | 0.6 | 0.6 | 0.7 | 0.7 | 0.6 |
| Economic services | 1.5 | 1.4 | 1.6 | 1.9 | 1.9 | 2.0 |
| Other | 4.8 | 4.4 | 4.1 | 5.3 | 5.7 | 5.3 |
| Gross investment | 4.1 | 3.1 | 3.8 | 3.9 | 3.6 | 2.9 |
| Taxes (per cent of GDP) | 39.8 | 45.0 | 46.9 | 47.8 | 48.0 | 47.9 |
| Direct taxes [1] | 15.8 | 16.9 | 18.0 | 18.0 | 17.3 | 15.7 |
| Indirect taxes | 13.6 | 15.5 | 15.1 | 15.2 | 15.0 | 14.9 |
| Compulsory fees, fines, etc. | 0.5 | 0.9 | 0.7 | 0.7 | 0.8 | 0.7 |
| Social security contributions | 9.9 | 11.6 | 13.0 | 13.9 | 14.9 | 16.5 |

|  | 1989 | 1990 | 1991 | 1992 | 1993 |
|---|---|---|---|---|---|
| **Tax rates (per cent)** | | | | | |
| Personal income tax | | | | | |
| State income tax | | | | | |
| Top marginal rate | 44 | 43 | 39 | 39 | 39 |
| Lowest marginal rate | 11 | 9 | 7 | 7 | 7 |
| Average local income tax | 16.3 | 16.5 | 16.6 | 16.8 | 17.2 |
| Social security contributions | | | | | |
| Employer's national pension and sickness<br>insurance | | | | | |
| Private | 5.74 | 5.32 | 3.58 | 3.35 | 3.85 |
| Public | 7.84 | 7.51 | 7.52 | 7.50 | 7.50 |
| Unemployment insurance | 0.85 | 0.60 | 1.40 | 3.70 | 6.00 |
| Insured persons | 3.25 | 3.25 | 3.25-4.25 | 3.25-4.75 [3] | |
| Value-added tax | 16 [2] | 17 | 17.5 /21.2 [4] | 22 | 22 |
| Corporate tax | 33 | 25 | 23 | 19 | 25 |
| Net wealth tax | | | | | |
| Top marginal rate | 0.9 | 0.9 | 0.9 | 0.9 | 0.9 |
| Lowest marginal rate | 0.9 | 0.9 | 0.9 | 0.9 | 0.9 |

1. Excluding so-called church tax.
2. 16.5 from 1 June and 17 from 1 December.
3. Dependent on income level.
4. Per cent of value of sale including tax. As of 1 October 1991, 22 per cent of sale, excluding tax.
*Source:* Submission from the Ministry of Finance.

*BASIC STATISTICS*

*BASIC STATISTICS:*

*INTERNATIONAL COMPARISONS*

| | Units | Reference period [1] | Australia | Austi |
|---|---|---|---|---|
| **Population** | | | | |
| Total | Thousands | 1992 | 17 489 | 7 8 |
| Inhabitants per sq. km | Number | 1992 | 2 | |
| Net average annual increase over previous 10 years | % | 1992 | 1.4 | 0 |
| **Employment** | | | | |
| Civilian employment (CE)[2] | Thousands | 1992 | 7 637 | 3 5 |
| Of which: Agriculture | % of CE | | 5.3 | 7 |
| Industry | % of CE | | 23.8 | 35 |
| Services | % of CE | | 71 | 57 |
| **Gross domestic product (GDP)** | | | | |
| At current prices and current exchange rates | Bill. US$ | 1992 | 296.6 | 186 |
| Per capita | US$ | | 16 959 | 23 6 |
| At current prices using current PPPs[3] | Bill. US$ | 1992 | 294.5 | 14 |
| Per capita | US$ | | 16 800 | 18 0 |
| Average annual volume growth over previous 5 years | % | 1992 | 2 | 3 |
| **Gross fixed capital formation (GFCF)** | % of GDP | 1992 | 19.7 | 2 |
| Of which: Machinery and equipment | % of GDP | | 9.3 | 9 |
| Residential construction | % of GDP | | 5.1 | 5 |
| Average annual volume growth over previous 5 years | % | 1992 | –1 | 5 |
| **Gross saving ratio[4]** | % of GDP | 1992 | 15.6 | 25 |
| **General government** | | | | |
| Current expenditure on goods and services | % of GDP | 1992 | 18.5 | 18. |
| Current disbursements[5] | % of GDP | 1992 | 36.9 | 46. |
| Current receipts | % of GDP | 1992 | 33.1 | 48. |
| **Net official development assistance** | % of GNP | 1992 | 0.33 | 0. |
| **Indicators of living standards** | | | | |
| Private consumption per capita using current PPPs[3] | US$ | 1992 | 10 527 | 9 95 |
| Passenger cars, per 1 000 inhabitants | Number | 1990 | 430 | 38 |
| Telephones, per 1 000 inhabitants | Number | 1990 | 448 | 58 |
| Television sets, per 1 000 inhabitants | Number | 1989 | 484 | 47 |
| Doctors, per 1 000 inhabitants | Number | 1991 | 2 | 2. |
| Infant mortality per 1 000 live births | Number | 1991 | 7.1 | 7. |
| **Wages and prices** (average annual increase over previous 5 years) | | | | |
| Wages (earnings or rates according to availability) | % | 1992 | 5 | 5. |
| Consumer prices | % | 1992 | 5.2 | |
| **Foreign trade** | | | | |
| Exports of goods, fob* | Mill. US$ | 1992 | 42 844 | 44 36 |
| As % of GDP | % | | 14.4 | 23. |
| Average annual increase over previous 5 years | % | | 10.1 | 10. |
| Imports of goods, cif* | Mill. US$ | 1992 | 40 751 | 54 03 |
| As % of GDP | % | | 13.7 | 2 |
| Average annual increase over previous 5 years | % | | 8.6 | 10. |
| **Total official reserves[6]** | Mill. SDRs | 1992 | 8 152 | 9 00 |
| As ratio of average monthly imports of goods | Ratio | | 2.4 | 2 |

* At current prices and exchange rates.
1. Unless otherwise stated.
2. According to the definitions used in OECD *Labour Force Statistics*.
3. PPPs = Purchasing Power Parities.
4. Gross saving = Gross national disposable income minus private and government consumption.
5. Current disbursements = Current expenditure on goods and services plus current transfers and payments of property income.
6. Gold included in reserves is valued at 35 SDRs per ounce. End of year.
7. Including Luxembourg.

# EMPLOYMENT OPPORTUNITIES

## *Economics Department, OECD*

The Economics Department of the OECD offers challenging and rewarding opportunities to economists interested in applied policy analysis in an international environment. The Department's concerns extend across the entire field of economic policy analysis, both macro-economic and micro-economic. Its main task is to provide, for discussion by committees of senior officials from Member countries, documents and papers dealing with current policy concerns. Within this programme of work, three major responsibilities are:

- to prepare regular surveys of the economies of individual Member countries;
- to issue full twice-yearly reviews of the economic situation and prospects of the OECD countries in the context of world economic trends;
- to analyse specific policy issues in a medium-term context for theOECD as a whole, and to a lesser extent for the non-OECD countries.

The documents prepared for these purposes, together with much of the Department's other economic work, appear in published form in the *OECD Economic Outlook, OECD Economic Surveys, OECD Economic Studies* and the Department's *Working Papers* series.

The Department maintains a world econometric model, INTERLINK, which plays an important role in the preparation of the policy analyses and twice-yearly projections. The availability of extensive cross-country data bases and good computer resources facilitates comparative empirical analysis, much of which is incorporated into the model.

The Department is made up of about 75 professional economists from a variety of backgrounds and Member countries. Most projects are carried out by small teams and last from four to eighteen months. Within the Department, ideas and points of view are widely discussed; there is a lively professional interchange, and all professional staff have the opportunity to contribute actively to the programme of work.

### Skills the Economics Department is looking for:

*a)* Solid competence in using the tools of both micro-economic and macro-economic theory to answer policy questions. Experience indicates that this normally requires the equivalent of a PH.D. in economics or substantial relevant professional experience to compensate for a lower degree.

*b)* Solid knowledge of economic statistics and quantitative methods; this includes how to identify data, estimate structural relationships, apply basic techniques of time series analysis, and test hypotheses. It is essential to be able to interpret results sensibly in an economic policy context.

*c)* A keen interest in and knowledge of policy issues, economic developments and their political/social contexts.

*d)* Interest and experience in analysing questions posed by policy-makers and presenting the results to them effectively and judiciously. Thus, work experience in government agencies or policy research institutions is an advantage.

*e)* The ability to write clearly, effectively, and to the point. The OECD is a bilingual organisation with French and English as the official languages. Candidates must have excellent knowledge of one of these languages, and some knowledge of the other. Knowledge of other languages might also be an advantage for certain posts.

*f)* For some posts, expertise in a particular area may be important, but a successful candidate is expected to be able to work on a broader range of topics relevant to the work of the Department. Thus, except in rare cases, the Department does not recruit narrow specialists.

*g)* The Department works on a tight time schedule and strict deadlines. Moreover, much of the work in the Department is carried out in small groups of economists. Thus, the ability to work with other economists from a variety of cultural and professional backgrounds, to supervise junior staff, and to produce work on time is important.

## General Information

The salary for recruits depends on educational and professional background. Positions carry a basic salary from FF 262 512 or FF 323 916 for Administrators (economists) and from FF 375 708 for Principal Administrators (senior economists). This may be supplemented by expatriation and/or family allowances, depending on nationality, residence and family situation. Initial appointments are for a fixed term of two to three years.

Vacancies are open to candidates from OECD Member countries. The Organisation seeks to maintain an appropriate balance between female and male staff and among nationals from Member countries.

For further information on employment opportunities in the Economics Department, contact:

**Administrative Unit**
**Economics Department**
**OECD**
**2, rue André-Pascal**
**75775 PARIS CEDEX 16**
**FRANCE**

Applications citing "ECSUR", together with a detailed *curriculum vitae* in English or French, should be sent to the Head of Personnel at the above address.

# MAIN SALES OUTLETS OF OECD PUBLICATIONS
# PRINCIPAUX POINTS DE VENTE DES PUBLICATIONS DE L'OCDE

**ARGENTINA – ARGENTINE**
Carlos Hirsch S.R.L.
Galería Güemes, Florida 165, 4° Piso
1333 Buenos Aires   Tel. (1) 331.1787 y 331.2391
                                    Telefax: (1) 331.1787

**AUSTRALIA – AUSTRALIE**
D.A. Information Services
648 Whitehorse Road, P.O.B 163
Mitcham, Victoria 3132        Tel. (03) 873.4411
                                       Telefax: (03) 873.5679

**AUSTRIA – AUTRICHE**
Gerold & Co.
Graben 31
Wien I                    Tel. (0222) 533.50.14

**BELGIUM – BELGIQUE**
Jean De Lannoy
Avenue du Roi 202
B-1060 Bruxelles   Tel. (02) 538.51.69/538.08.41
                              Telefax: (02) 538.08.41

**CANADA**
Renouf Publishing Company Ltd.
1294 Algoma Road
Ottawa, ON K1B 3W8        Tel. (613) 741.4333
                                     Telefax: (613) 741.5439
Stores:
61 Sparks Street
Ottawa, ON K1P 5R1        Tel. (613) 238.8985
211 Yonge Street
Toronto, ON M5B 1M4        Tel. (416) 363.3171
                                     Telefax: (416)363.59.63

Les Éditions La Liberté Inc.
3020 Chemin Sainte-Foy
Sainte-Foy, PQ G1X 3V6      Tel. (418) 658.3763
                                     Telefax: (418) 658.3763

Federal Publications Inc.
165 University Avenue, Suite 701
Toronto, ON M5H 3B8        Tel. (416) 860.1611
                                     Telefax: (416) 860.1608

Les Publications Fédérales
1185 Université
Montréal, QC H3B 3A7        Tel. (514) 954.1633
                                     Telefax : (514) 954.1635

**CHINA – CHINE**
China National Publications Import
Export Corporation (CNPIEC)
16 Gongti E. Road, Chaoyang District
P.O. Box 88 or 50
Beijing 100704 PR        Tel. (01) 506.6688
                                  Telefax: (01) 506.3101

**DENMARK – DANEMARK**
Munksgaard Book and Subscription Service
35, Nørre Søgade, P.O. Box 2148
DK-1016 København K      Tel. (33) 12.85.70
                                    Telefax: (33) 12.93.87

**FINLAND – FINLANDE**
Akateeminen Kirjakauppa
Keskuskatu 1, P.O. Box 128
00100 Helsinki
Subscription Services/Agence d'abonnements :
P.O. Box 23
00371 Helsinki          Tel. (358 0) 12141
                                  Telefax: (358 0) 121.4450

**FRANCE**
OECD/OCDE
Mail Orders/Commandes par correspondance:
2, rue André-Pascal
75775 Paris Cedex 16        Tel. (33-1) 45.24.82.00
                                      Telefax: (33-1) 49.10.42.76
                                      Telex: 640048 OCDE
Orders via Minitel, France only/
Commandes par Minitel, France exclusivement :
36 15 OCDE

OECD Bookshop/Librairie de l'OCDE :
33, rue Octave-Feuillet
75016 Paris            Tel. (33-1) 45.24.81.67
                                  (33-1) 45.24.81.81

Documentation Française
29, quai Voltaire
75007 Paris            Tel. 40.15.70.00

Gibert Jeune (Droit-Économie)
6, place Saint-Michel
75006 Paris            Tel. 43.25.91.19

Librairie du Commerce International
10, avenue d'Iéna
75016 Paris            Tel. 40.73.34.60

Librairie Dunod
Université Paris-Dauphine
Place du Maréchal de Lattre de Tassigny
75016 Paris            Tel. (1) 44.05.40.13

Librairie Lavoisier
11, rue Lavoisier
75008 Paris            Tel. 42.65.39.95

Librairie L.G.D.J. - Montchrestien
20, rue Soufflot
75005 Paris            Tel. 46.33.89.85

Librairie des Sciences Politiques
30, rue Saint-Guillaume
75007 Paris            Tel. 45.48.36.02

P.U.F.
49, boulevard Saint-Michel
75005 Paris            Tel. 43.25.83.40

Librairie de l'Université
12a, rue Nazareth
13100 Aix-en-Provence    Tel. (16) 42.26.18.08

Documentation Française
165, rue Garibaldi
69003 Lyon            Tel. (16) 78.63.32.23

Librairie Decitre
29, place Bellecour
69002 Lyon            Tel. (16) 72.40.54.54

**GERMANY – ALLEMAGNE**
OECD Publications and Information Centre
August-Bebel-Allee 6
D-53175 Bonn            Tel. (0228) 959.120
                                  Telefax: (0228) 959.12.17

**GREECE – GRÈCE**
Librairie Kauffmann
Mavrokordatou 9
106 78 Athens          Tel. (01) 32.55.321
                                  Telefax: (01) 36.33.967

**HONG-KONG**
Swindon Book Co. Ltd.
13–15 Lock Road
Kowloon, Hong Kong    Tel. 366.80.31
                                  Telefax: 739.49.75

**HUNGARY – HONGRIE**
Euro Info Service
Margitsziget, Európa Ház
1138 Budapest          Tel. (1) 111.62.16
                                  Telefax : (1) 111.60.61

**ICELAND – ISLANDE**
Mál Mog Menning
Laugavegi 18, Pósthólf 392
121 Reykjavik          Tel. 162.35.23

**INDIA – INDE**
Oxford Book and Stationery Co.
Scindia House
New Delhi 110001        Tel.(11) 331.5896/5308
                                  Telefax: (11) 332.5993
17 Park Street
Calcutta 700016        Tel. 240832

**INDONESIA – INDONÉSIE**
Pdii-Lipi
P.O. Box 269/JKSMG/88
Jakarta 12790          Tel. 583467
                                  Telex: 62 875

**ISRAEL**
Praedicta
5 Shatner Street
P.O. Box 34030
Jerusalem 91430        Tel. (2) 52.84.90/1/2
                                  Telefax: (2) 52.84.93

R.O.Y.
P.O. Box 13056
Tel Aviv 61130          Tél. (3) 49.61.08
                                  Telefax (3) 544.60.39

**ITALY – ITALIE**
Libreria Commissionaria Sansoni
Via Duca di Calabria 1/1
50125 Firenze          Tel. (055) 64.54.15
                                  Telefax: (055) 64.12.57
Via Bartolini 29
20155 Milano          Tel. (02) 36.50.83
Editrice e Libreria Herder
Piazza Montecitorio 120
00186 Roma            Tel. 679.46.28
                                  Telefax: 678.47.51
Libreria Hoepli
Via Hoepli 5
20121 Milano          Tel. (02) 86.54.46
                                  Telefax: (02) 805.28.86
Libreria Scientifica
Dott. Lucio de Biasio 'Aeiou'
Via Coronelli, 6
20146 Milano          Tel. (02) 48.95.45.52
                                  Telefax: (02) 48.95.45.48

**JAPAN – JAPON**
OECD Publications and Information Centre
Landic Akasaka Building
2-3-4 Akasaka, Minato-ku
Tokyo 107              Tel. (81.3) 3586.2016
                                  Telefax: (81.3) 3584.7929

**KOREA – CORÉE**
Kyobo Book Centre Co. Ltd.
P.O. Box 1658, Kwang Hwa Moon
Seoul                  Tel. 730.78.91
                                  Telefax: 735.00.30

**MALAYSIA – MALAISIE**
Co-operative Bookshop Ltd.
University of Malaya
P.O. Box 1127, Jalan Pantai Baru
59700 Kuala Lumpur
Malaysia                Tel. 756.5000/756.5425
                                  Telefax: 757.3661

**MEXICO – MEXIQUE**
Revistas y Periodicos Internacionales S.A. de C.V.
Florencia 57 - 1004
Mexico, D.F. 06600        Tel. 207.81.00
                                  Telefax : 208.39.79

**NETHERLANDS – PAYS-BAS**
SDU Uitgeverij Plantijnstraat
Externe Fondsen
Postbus 20014
2500 EA's-Gravenhage    Tel. (070) 37.89.880
Voor bestellingen:        Telefax: (070) 34.75.778

**NEW ZEALAND**
**NOUVELLE-ZÉLANDE**
Legislation Services
P.O. Box 12418
Thorndon, Wellington          Tel. (04) 496.5652
                         Telefax: (04) 496.5698

**NORWAY – NORVÈGE**
Narvesen Info Center – NIC
Bertrand Narvesens vei 2
P.O. Box 6125 Etterstad
0602 Oslo 6                   Tel. (022) 57.33.00
                         Telefax: (022) 68.19.01

**PAKISTAN**
Mirza Book Agency
65 Shahrah Quaid-E-Azam
Lahore 54000                  Tel. (42) 353.601
                         Telefax: (42) 231.730

**PHILIPPINE – PHILIPPINES**
International Book Center
5th Floor, Filipinas Life Bldg.
Ayala Avenue
Metro Manila                  Tel. 81.96.76
                         Telex 23312 RHP PH

**PORTUGAL**
Livraria Portugal
Rua do Carmo 70-74
Apart. 2681
1200 Lisboa                   Tel.: (01) 347.49.82/5
                         Telefax: (01) 347.02.64

**SINGAPORE – SINGAPOUR**
Gower Asia Pacific Pte Ltd.
Golden Wheel Building
41, Kallang Pudding Road, No. 04-03
Singapore 1334                Tel. 741.5166
                         Telefax: 742.9356

**SPAIN – ESPAGNE**
Mundi-Prensa Libros S.A.
Castelló 37, Apartado 1223
Madrid 28001                  Tel. (91) 431.33.99
                         Telefax: (91) 575.39.98

Libreria Internacional AEDOS
Consejo de Ciento 391
08009 – Barcelona             Tel. (93) 488.30.09
                         Telefax: (93) 487.76.59
Llibreria de la Generalitat
Palau Moja
Rambla dels Estudis, 118
08002 – Barcelona
            (Subscripcions) Tel. (93) 318.80.12
            (Publicacions) Tel. (93) 302.67.23
                         Telefax: (93) 412.18.54

**SRI LANKA**
Centre for Policy Research
c/o Colombo Agencies Ltd.
No. 300-304, Galle Road
Colombo 3          Tel. (1) 574240, 573551-2
                         Telefax: (1) 575394, 510711

**SWEDEN – SUÈDE**
Fritzes Information Center
Box 16356
Regeringsgatan 12
106 47 Stockholm              Tel. (08) 690.90.90
                         Telefax: (08) 20.50.21
Subscription Agency/Agence d'abonnements :
Wennergren-Williams Info AB
P.O. Box 1305
171 25 Solna                  Tel. (08) 705.97.50
                         Téléfax : (08) 27.00.71

**SWITZERLAND – SUISSE**
Maditec S.A. (Books and Periodicals - Livres
et périodiques)
Chemin des Palettes 4
Case postale 266
1020 Renens                   Tel. (021) 635.08.65
                         Telefax: (021) 635.07.80

Librairie Payot S.A.
4, place Pépinet
CP 3212
1002 Lausanne                 Tel. (021) 341.33.48
                         Telefax: (021) 341.33.45

Librairie Unilivres
6, rue de Candolle
1205 Genève                   Tel. (022) 320.26.23
                         Telefax: (022) 329.73.18

Subscription Agency/Agence d'abonnements :
Dynapresse Marketing S.A.
38 avenue Vibert
1227 Carouge                  Tel.: (022) 308.07.89
                         Telefax : (022) 308.07.99

See also – Voir aussi :
OECD Publications and Information Centre
August-Bebel-Allee 6
D-53175 Bonn (Germany)        Tel. (0228) 959.120
                         Telefax: (0228) 959.12.17

**TAIWAN – FORMOSE**
Good Faith Worldwide Int'l. Co. Ltd.
9th Floor, No. 118, Sec. 2
Chung Hsiao E. Road
Taipei              Tel. (02) 391.7396/391.7397
                         Telefax: (02) 394.9176

**THAILAND – THAÏLANDE**
Suksit Siam Co. Ltd.
113, 115 Fuang Nakhon Rd.
Opp. Wat Rajbopith
Bangkok 10200                 Tel. (662) 225.9531/2
                         Telefax: (662) 222.5188

**TURKEY – TURQUIE**
Kültür Yayinlari Is-Türk Ltd. Sti.
Atatürk Bulvari No. 191/Kat 13
Kavaklidere/Ankara      Tel. 428.11.40 Ext. 2458
Dolmabahce Cad. No. 29
Besiktas/Istanbul             Tel. 260.71.88
                         Telex: 43482B

**UNITED KINGDOM – ROYAUME-UNI**
HMSO
Gen. enquiries                Tel. (071) 873 0011
Postal orders only:
P.O. Box 276, London SW8 5DT
Personal Callers HMSO Bookshop
49 High Holborn, London WC1V 6HB
                         Telefax: (071) 873 8200
Branches at: Belfast, Birmingham, Bristol, Edin-
burgh, Manchester

**UNITED STATES – ÉTATS-UNIS**
OECD Publications and Information Centre
2001 L Street N.W., Suite 700
Washington, D.C. 20036-4910 Tel. (202) 785.6323
                         Telefax: (202) 785.0350

**VENEZUELA**
Libreria del Este
Avda F. Miranda 52, Aptdo. 60337
Edificio Galipán
Caracas 106    Tel. 951.1705/951.2307/951.1297
                         Telegram: Libreste Caracas

Subscription to OECD periodicals may also be
placed through main subscription agencies.

Les abonnements aux publications périodiques de
l'OCDE peuvent être souscrits auprès des
principales agences d'abonnement.

Orders and inquiries from countries where Distribu-
tors have not yet been appointed should be sent to:
OECD Publications Service, 2 rue André-Pascal,
75775 Paris Cedex 16, France.

Les commandes provenant de pays où l'OCDE n'a
pas encore désigné de distributeur peuvent être
adressées à : OCDE, Service des Publications,
2, rue André-Pascal, 75775 Paris Cedex 16, France.

11-1994

PRINTED IN FRANCE

●

OECD PUBLICATIONS
2, rue André-Pascal
75775 PARIS CEDEX 16
No. 47633
(10 95 31 1) ISBN 92-64-14336-X
ISSN 0376-6438

●